THIS
BELOVED
ROAD

THIS BELOVED ROAD

A Journey of Revelation and Worship

Amy Layne Litzelman

TATE PUBLISHING & Enterprises

Published by Tate Publishing & Enterprises, LLC
127 E. Trade Center Terrace | Mustang, Oklahoma 73064 USA
1.888.361.9473 | www.tatepublishing.com

Tate Publishing is committed to excellence in the publishing industry. The company reflects the philosophy established by the founders, based on Psalm 68:11,
"The Lord gave the word and great was the company of those who published it."

Book design copyright © 2010 by Tate Publishing, LLC. All rights reserved.
Cover design and Interior design by Blake Brasor

Published in the United States of America
ISBN: 978-1-61739-083-8
1. Religion, Christian Life, Devotional
2. Religion, Christian Life, Spiritual Growth
10.08.16

Table of Contents

Introduction

I don't recall the exact date, although I could probably search through journals and find it. I distinctly remember the moment, however. Something reached off the page and grabbed my heart as I read Jeremiah 20:9 (AMP), "If I say, I will not make mention of [the Lord] or speak any more in His name, in my mind and heart it is as if there were a burning fire shut up in my bones. And I am weary of enduring it and holding it in; I cannot [contain it any longer]."

I stopped short, hardly able to breathe. I read and re-read this verse, seeing something I was starving for yet didn't quite know how to get. I wanted *that* fire—an uncontainable fire. I wanted to be overcome with it. So I did all I knew to do. I began to ask for it, yearn for it, run after it. I soon discovered, however, that this fire—this unquenchable presence of God—had been pursuing me as much as I now pursued it.

Amy Layne, the names given to me at birth, mean "beloved road." I didn't always know what my name meant, and I certainly didn't always think my life went down a beloved path. But as I pursued a God who had so captured my heart that just speaking his name made me smile, I began to see that I was growing into a name that I believe he gave my parents to give to me. Every step, every moment, was one more I could spend with the one who loved me more than I could ever understand and who longed for my love in return.

This collection of eighty columns and songs follows several years of pressing in to know my Father's heart and experiencing his gentle, life-changing responses. It records a discovery of irreplaceable friendship, unyielding love, unwavering forgiveness, insistent perseverance, and grace beyond all reasoning. This fire has truly become my consuming passion: to know the one who knows me, the one who has burned his love on my heart—to know him and to be one with him. I cannot contain it any longer.

No Gimmicks

Tax collectors and other notorious sinners often came to listen
to Jesus teach.

Luke 15:1 (NLT)

This verse caught my eye. What an amazing testimony to the truth
of who Jesus was, and is, and the life which he carries. Life-giving
words poured out, and those who were dry and dead recognized it.
He didn't have schemes or gimmicks. He had life.

I want to be like that. I want my Father's life to be so full in me
that it draws those who need it. I want the "me" to be so covered
with him that I find myself surrounded by seekers—seekers of truth,
seekers of life.

A lot of things in this world offer an abundant lifestyle, but there
is only one true source for abundant life itself. And there is only one
way to truly answer the needs in those around us. We must have this
life surging out of us every day, everywhere we go.

Amy Layne Litzelman

So Did You Lead

Like the cattle that go down into the valley [to find better pasturage, refuge, and rest], the Spirit of the Lord caused them to rest. So did You lead Your people [Lord] to make for Yourself a beautiful and glorious name [to prepare the way for the acknowledgement of Your name by all nations.

Isaiah 63:14 (AMP)

As I look across the many layers of hills and mountains surrounding my home in Jackson Hole, Wyoming, I am reminded that there are also many hills and mountains in the Spirit, with so many varying paths up each.

There is such an unfathomable depth to our Father. Romans 11:33 states his ways, methods, and paths are mysterious and untraceable. He alone knows the exact, perfect design of revealing himself to each of us. Just as we will never climb every physical mountain, we will never be able to climb every spiritual mountain. And even if we climb the same mountain as someone else, we will probably take different routes. God never teaches his truths and secrets in the same order, timing, or way to any two people. He delights in speaking to and directing us individually.

While this is an exciting thought, it can also lead to frustration with those around us. We want others to do it like we do it, or to be in the same place of understanding that we are. Or maybe just the opposite; maybe we look around and wish we were on someone else's path. But, like pieces of an intricate puzzle, our Lord places us in just the perfect place for his perfect plan. The one thing that we can *always* encourage each other with is the steady, unfailing, unchanging character of God: his goodness, his wisdom, his power, and his faithfulness. These never waver or change no matter what path we are on.

In great wisdom and care, God directs us in such a way as to bring glory to his name—to cause the nations to stand in awe of him. Where are you walking today? What path is he leading you down? Do you know that in that *very* place exists the potential for great and glorious things?

The Most Perfect Place

For thus said the Lord God, the Holy One of Israel: In returning [to Me] and resting [in Me] you shall be saved; in quietness and in [trusting] confidence shall be your strength...

Isaiah 30:15 (AMP)

It's funny how God is so overwhelmingly sovereign and majestic and yet so real. As I read several different verses about resting in him, I said in my mind, *Yes, Father, I know that.* And he said, *No, you really don't know it, but by the end of today you will know it better.*

And so he began to take me deeper into the verse above. The only place we are saved is in him. But to truly be in him is to be in a place of total trust and confidence in who he is. If we are sliding around in worry or frustration, we may be somewhere close to him, but we aren't resting in him.

Now, I'm not talking about our eternal salvation. We all have bad days or moments, but our salvation is still sure. What I'm talking about is being saved every single day from the restlessness and anxiety of the world around us. God wants to lead us to a place of assurance where we *know* that we can relax and lean back in to him because we know how much he loves us—how much we can trust every plan he has for us, every word of direction he speaks to us.

A certain quietness comes over us as we get a deeper revelation of just how much we can trust God. An amazing confidence goes to our very core. Not a shallow, external confidence that still expects some degree of error or weakness. Rather, it is a place of being able to lean our entire heart, mind, soul, and being on Jesus—a true place of rest.

No, I still don't know as much as I will by next week or next year, but I'm learning that resting is an amazing thing. Resting in Christ and his love for me, personally and individually, is the most prefect place I've ever been. And he's not supposed to be a vacation spot. He is home.

Threshold Living

As God has said: I will dwell in them and walk among them. I will be their God and they shall be my people. Therefore, come out from among them and be separate, says the Lord. Do not touch what is unclean and I will receive you. I will be a Father to you, and you shall be my sons and daughters, says the Lord Almighty.

Therefore, having these promises, beloved, let us cleanse ourselves from all filthiness of flesh and spirit, perfecting holiness in the fear of God.

2 Corinthians 6:16b-7:1 (NKJV)

It is not a new concept that we should be different than the world around us, but the Holy Spirit gave me another simple picture of what that really looks like. I was sitting in the doorway between my living room and patio. Outside it was hot and the bugs were everywhere. Inside the house was cool and comfortable. As I sat with the door open, a giant, black fly buzzed by my head and into the house. Immediately, the Spirit began to teach me. The outside patio was a picture of being in the world, unsheltered from the elements, where the nuisance, distraction, and attacks of spiritual darkness (bugs) had free reign. Inside the house represented being in the hidden presence of God, shielded and protected. Although most of me was in the house, my feet were outside and the door was wide open for the bugs to invade my home.

As I asked to see what God saw, he showed me a specific area where my feet were in the world, where I was thinking and acting like the world instead of how Christ would think or act. Repentance put me back under the covering of his wings and closed the door to the outside. However, there was still the need to deal with the "flies" that had come into the house through my carelessness. By submitting to and washing in the Word, I had soon taken the right away from Satan to attack specific areas of my life.

Was it a huge issue of disobedience? No. In fact, it was really pretty silly to most peoples' thinking. My husband, Matt, and I had recently purchased a zippy, little car after driving a large pick-up truck for years. I hadn't been in an accident or gotten a ticket. No drinking and driving. But within no time I had taken on this zippy, little attitude whenever I drove out of the driveway; a seed of pride in this image of myself had fallen on fertile ground. It seems small, but small seeds grow into giant trees. What an amazing Father we have to point out seeds to us, instead of waiting until we have to figure out how to get that giant tree out of our living room.

The Fire of God

He will sit as a refiner and purifier of silver, and He will purify
the priests, the sons of Levi, and refine them like gold and silver,
that they may offer to the Lord offerings in righteousness.

Malachi 3:3 (AMP)

Have you ever seen a sunset when there is smoke in the air? Forest fires are common in the mountains of Wyoming and sometimes smoke just hangs in the valley, making visibility and breathing more difficult. But, oh, the sunsets. There's nothing like it!

A friend mentioned hearing a report on why forest fires are such a problem. Because of poor forest management, including not allowing smaller fires to thin out some areas, trees are now growing very large and dense; few new plants and undergrowth are able to live. Then, when we are faced with larger fires, these areas burn extremely hot, sometimes sterilizing the ground and stripping away important minerals.

As I marveled at a gorgeous sunset through the haze and thought about all of this, the Spirit reminded me of the effect of fire in our spiritual lives. Hebrews 12:29 states that our God is a consuming fire, and 1 Corinthians 3:13 reminds us that all we do will be tested with fire, revealing whether it be gold, silver, and precious stones or wood, hay, and stubble. With great love and care, God longs to burn up the old, dry, empty things in our lives, things that keep new growth from occurring. We can submit to his wisdom, confident that what is pure and eternal will not be consumed, or we can quench his fire when it gets too warm, letting our forest grow up around us.

There is a whole different realm of beauty and color when the sun shines through fire and smoke. And there is an uncommon beauty in people who submit to the fire of God. Sometimes those around them can't put a finger on it, but there is something—a fragrance of offering, a new depth of color—which pleases even the creator of the universe.

Fire will come; it's inevitable. But will it be a flame unto beauty, or of intense destruction? Trust his love. Trust his wisdom. God's fire burns but for a time, guided by his hand, and leaves his glory as the jewel in the ashes.

Hidden in Weakness

Trust (lean on, rely on, and be confident) in the Lord and do good; so shall you dwell in the land and feed surely on His faithfulness, and truly you shall be fed.

Psalm 37:3 (AMP)

On a hillside where I often take early morning hikes, I sat down to talk with God. After only a few minutes, I heard a rustle and turned to see a very large badger coming straight toward me, just a few feet away through the grass. Knowing their antagonistic reputation and my vulnerable position, I immediately braced myself, feeling my chest tighten. But just as immediate, I heard my Father say, *Sit still. He doesn't know you're here.*

Later, as I pondered that scene again, the Spirit explained that there is a place where the enemy, though right beside us, doesn't really see us; he is preoccupied with other things and unaware of our presence. But this place of hiddenness doesn't always look like we imagine it to.

When we think of being hidden in the stronghold of God, we often see ourselves as large, powerful, and robust, standing firmly with magnificent armor. And, sometimes, this is true. But the picture I saw this time was quite different. I was weak, weary, and exhausted. I appeared, from all exterior views, to be failing in several areas of my life, not handling certain situations as I longed to handle them.

I thought of Jesus and how he must have appeared the days and hours before his death. Again, from all exterior views, he seemed to be failing; he was weak, bloody, beaten, and broken. But in reality, he was in a place of which his enemy knew not—a place of incredible hiddenness—a place of supernatural strength. How?

You see, the adversary focuses on the outside, the obvious. He looks at our flesh and exterior circumstances and is quite content when we appear defeated in our human bodies. But our Lord knows all things; nothing is hidden from his eyes. Behind the curtain of our weakness, he is perfecting and pouring out his strength. Through our weaknesses, he is building his kingdom.

Paul was in a place of great frustration and pain, tormented by Satan and crying out to his God for relief when he heard the Spirit say, "My power works best in your weakness." What was Paul's response? "So now I am glad to boast about my weaknesses, so that the power of Christ may work through me" (2 Corinthians 12:9, NLT). The Amplified Bible says it this way, "Therefore, I will all the more gladly glory in my weaknesses and infirmities, that the strength and power of Christ may rest (yes, may pitch a tent over and dwell) upon me!"

Don't beat yourself up for being weak. Don't try to run from trials and infirmities. Instead, let the Spirit show you what only he sees, the hidden reality. Trust God's wisdom. Lean on him and be confident in his plans and purposes. Set your love upon him, for he is doing a work we could never imagine. We are standing in a land where we can feast upon his faithfulness. Let him pitch a tent of power and strength over you.

Sing to Him a New Song

Sing to Him a new song; play skillfully [on the strings] with a loud and joyful sound.

Psalm 33:3 (AMP)

Amy Layne Litzelman

Our God is vast. There is just no way around it. There is absolutely nothing small or insignificant about him. Isaiah 66:1 states that heaven is his throne and earth, his footstool. Job 36:26 (NLT) says, "Look, God is greater than we can understand. His years cannot be counted," and Job 37:5 (NLT) says, "God's voice is glorious in the thunder. We can't even imagine the greatness of his power."

One of my favorite verses (Hebrews 1:3, AMP) tells us that Jesus—the sole expression of the glory of God—upholds, maintains, guides, and propels the universe by his mighty word of power!

He laid the foundations of the earth and set the boundaries of the sea. The morning stars sing his praise, as do the earth and all that is in it. By his breath the waters are frozen, and on his word clouds move across the sky and release their rain.

Our God calls forth life from the womb, restores the years the locusts have eaten, and causes nations to scatter. He is our judge, our king, our father, our friend, and our beloved.

His beauty is at the same time dazzling and soft. His love releases both weeping of repentance and joy. His faithfulness is crucial to our existence, for even when we are faithless, he is faithful. He could have no greater love for us, no deeper commitment, and no stronger tie. His relationship overshadows all others.

When we are utterly forsaken, completely broken, totally filthy, and undone, he calls us to himself and covers us in his kindness. He feeds us, clothes us, comforts us, and sustains us. He guides, shields, protects, and establishes us.

Job 36:5 (AMP) proclaims, "Behold! God is mighty, and yet despises no one nor regards anything as trivial; He is mighty in power of understanding and heart."

What kind of marvelous God do we serve? One who will take a lifetime plus eternity to know. One who deserves unending praise and adoration.

As a musician and song writer, sometimes the thought goes through my head that so very many songs have been written—surely there are no more to write. Then I spend a moment or an hour or a day with my God, and my heart swells with words and rhythms, revealing again to me how vast he truly is!

Sing to him a new song.

It's All About Trust

> The Lord is my Strength and my [impenetrable] Shield; my heart trusts in, relies on, and confidently leans on Him, and I am helped; therefore my heart greatly rejoices, and with my song will I praise Him.
>
> Psalm 28:7 (AMP)

God has given all of us a measure of faith, and from the time we are young, all through our lives, we choose what to put our faith in—what to trust in. Either our faith grows because we find what we are trusting in is worthy of that trust, or it decreases and shifts to something else. But all of this happens through tests and trials.

The more I open myself up to know God, the more I know how important this issue really is. It is so important, in fact, that every moment of every day offers another chance to learn the depths of his unending trustworthiness.

When I was a young Christian, I had the faith of a child. I had a simple love and non-questioning faith. I simply believed without asking questions because I had experienced God's grace and mercy, and that was perfectly appropriate for that time in my life (Luke 18:17.) Then I grew and life became more complicated, and not everything made immediate sense. So I started asking more questions. I started questioning why and how certain things could happen when I knew God to be this large, loving Father. I was on a journey and didn't even know it. I was on a road marked with lessons in God's character and motivation.

James 1:2–3 exhorts us to be joyful on this journey filled with trials and temptations, knowing that these difficulties will actually prove and strengthen our faith, giving us endurance and steadfastness.

I think of Jesus. He entered both the world and the kingdom as a child. He grew in wisdom and stature and in favor with God and man. He was tempted and tried in every area. In all this, Jesus's trust in his Father was so total and so strong that even as he sweated drops of blood at the thought of what was before him, he submitted to the purpose of the crucifixion, knowing he could trust God with the outcome.

As my faith is tested and strengthened, I am able to trust my Father with things I never would have imagined a few years ago, but he never stops asking me to trust him again, to another, deeper place. He wants me to know, again, the depths of his love. Although this may cause a mixture of feelings and emotions, there comes a point on a journey where there is no turning back. I have seen enough and experienced enough to know I am on the right road. I have tasted his goodness. I am utterly convinced of his kindness and wisdom. I may not understand all that is in front of me, but I understand this: his way is the only perfect way.

Amy Layne Litzelman

The Whole Duty of Man

Now all has been heard; here is the conclusion of the matter:
Fear God and keep his commandments, for this is the whole
duty of man.

Ecclesiastes 12:13 (NIV)

When our son, Samuel, was twelve years old, Matt and I were asked
to answer the following question: As parents, what do you want your
son to become as an adult? What a huge question. So many things
ran through our minds. Having lived almost four decades, some in
God's will and some not, we asked the Spirit for the perfect words
to express what he wanted for our son. Ecclesiastes 12:13 is where we
ended up. The Amplified Translation puts it this way:

All has been heard; the end of the matter is: Fear God
[revere and worship Him, knowing that He is] and keep His
commandments, for this is the whole of man [the full, original
purpose of His creation, the object of God's providence, the root
of character, the foundation of all happiness, the adjustment to
all inharmonious circumstances and conditions under the sun]
and the whole [duty] for every man.

As I thought about these two directives, I realized the importance
of the combination; we need both reverence and obedience. If we
worship but do not walk in obedience and discipline, we are emo-
tional, lacking self-control and godly character. If we obey God's
commandments but are not true worshipers, we become religious
and judgmental. As the Pharisees in Jesus's day, we may miss the real
meaning and purpose, even God himself.

Jesus said true worshipers worship in Spirit and in truth. Authentic reverence and worship is not something we can just make happen. We must receive a Spirit-given understanding of God, a Spirit-revelation of his goodness. How? Ask. Seek. Knock. And as we get glimpse after glimpse of the incredible greatness of our God, we worship. It just happens, deep unto deep.

Obedience, on the other hand, is something we make happen. Each and every day is full of choices—choices which he will not make for us—choices between his way and our way. After standing in that place of revelation and seeing the stunning contrast between God and ourselves, we must choose whether or not to let him change us into his image and character.

So, what do we want our son to be? One who knows God in all of the passion and revelation available through the Spirit, and who then chooses to be conformed into his likeness through an obedient lifestyle. This is the glory of God in earthen vessels.

What Makes You Content

Let them give thanks to the Lord for his unfailing love and his wonderful deeds for men, for he satisfies the thirsty and fills the hungry with good things.

Psalm 107:8–9 (NIV)

What makes you content? Is it the people you are with, the place you are visiting, or the activity in which you are engaged? Or is it a random emotion or feeling?

I had come to the end of a busy day and was in need of some silence—a rare commodity in a home with two young sons. Funny as it may seem, I went out and sat in the car, in the driveway, as a solution. As I just spent time talking to God, I asked if he was pleased with me. His soft, gentle answer was, *No*. It wasn't at all painful to hear. When I asked why, he said, *Because you are not content.*

Now, I have learned over and over not to be afraid of God's answers; they come with such love and hope. So, as I mulled this over, he opened my understanding to see what he meant. Although my day had been full of the love and grace of God, and I had seen his hand moving constantly, by dinnertime I had allowed my physical weariness to steal away my joy. Instead of focusing on the consistency of his goodness and favor, I was noticing all the dreary details of the evening chores. I was not content.

Funk and Wagnalls Standard Desk Dictionary defines *contented* as "satisfied with things as they are."[1] There is only one way to be satisfied, regardless of the circumstances in which we find ourselves:

to focus our eyes and heart on things above. How was Paul able to proclaim that he was content in whatever state he found himself (Philippians 4:11)? He was empowered—infused—by Christ, himself, to see beyond this earthly realm. He chose to look upon God's goodness filling and surrounding his life.

God's glory, God's goodness, is everywhere if we simply have eyes to see it. In every little detail of our day, his love, wisdom, and power are revealed. Ask for eyes to see. Ask for a heart to recognize. Ask, and you will never lack for contentment.

I'm a Branch

I am the Vine; you are the branches. Whoever lives in Me and I in him bears much (abundant) fruit...

John 15:5 (AMP)

What a wonderful thought: *I am a branch.* And what an amazing promise: "Those who remain in me, and I in them, will produce much fruit" (NLT).

It seems that most of the time when I hear teaching on John 15, the focus is on the pruning. And, yes, pruning is a vital part of being a branch. But beyond the pruning, the purpose is fruit. Our future in Christ is so full of hope and promise. Ephesians 5:9 promises that the light of God will produce in us every form of goodness, truth, and uprightness of heart. Sometimes we are just going along, day to day, loving God, and obeying one step at a time. Then, suddenly, we look up and see ripe fruit in our lives we didn't even know was there. This fruit could be a change in attitude, a new compassion, deeper faith, greater wisdom, or less interest in the things of the world.

Psalm 92:12–15 (AMP) boldly proclaims:

> The [uncompromisingly] righteous shall flourish like the palm tree [be long-lived, stately, upright, useful, and fruitful]; they shall grow like a cedar in Lebanon [majestic, stable, durable, and incorruptible]. Planted in the house of the Lord, they shall flourish in the courts of our God. [Growing in grace] they shall still bring forth fruit in old age; they shall be full of sap [of spiritual vitality] and [rich in the] verdure [of trust, love and contentment]. [They are living memorials] to show that the Lord is upright and faithful to His promises...

What an outlook! When we remain in Christ and his life flows through us, we will bear fruit. Change will happen. Our Father will be greatly glorified. Thank you, Father, for this abundant life.

This Beloved Road

The path of the righteous is like the first gleam of dawn, shining
ever brighter till the full light of day.

Proverbs 4:18 (NIV)

Where you lead, I want to go
No matter what, I always know
Your way is straight, the perfect plan
Through meadows green or desert sand

Sometimes we dance, sometimes we crawl
But even when to my knees I fall
I weep for joy and rise again
With strength and love from your right hand

Oh this sweet beloved road
It leads me back to my true home
I'll hold your hand, I won't let go
While we walk on this beloved road

Lead me on, oh lead me out
To the places that we've talked about
Anywhere you want to go
Jesus, Master, lead me on

Take away all doubt and fear
As unfamiliar land we near
Just speak my name and I'll recall
You have walked this way before

Oh, this sweet beloved road
It leads me back to my true home
I'll hold your hand, I won't let go
While we walk on this beloved road

Prayer of Thanksgiving

For God so greatly loved and dearly prized the world that He
[even] gave up His only begotten (unique) Son, so that whoever
believes in (trusts in, clings to, relies on) Him shall not perish
(come to destruction, be lost) but have eternal (everlasting) life.

John 3:16 (AMP)

And this is eternal life: [it means] to know (to perceive, recognize,
become acquainted with and understand) You, the only true and
real God, and [likewise] to know Him, Jesus [as the] Christ,
(the Anointed One, the Messiah), whom You have sent.

John 17:3 (AMP)

Father, thank you for the eternal life you have given me. It is not a
gift we open after we die. It is poured in and upon us the moment
we trust, cling, rely, believe. No man can fully understand or grasp it
except in brilliant pieces, over and over again.

Thank you for your Son. Thank you for your Spirit. Thank you
for the security I have found in you.

I hear the ocean of your voice roaring inside me. I feel the thunder of your presence vibrating in my soul. I know the stability of the
truth on which I stand and I am again shaken to my depths. You are
beyond words. You are beyond all human thoughts can contain.

Stretch my thoughts. Stretch my mind. Open me up. Open my
understanding to know you more, my God and Father. Let me see
as you see. Let me love as you love. Let me be as you are, even a true
ambassador.

Oh holy Father, let me grasp anew the depths of your love. Let
me see afresh the heights of your thoughts. Let me taste again the

sweetness of you, knowing you never change. Deepen my love. Widen my perspective. Broaden my understanding. Don't leave me in this place, although it is one of great splendor. Take me deeper into your chambers. Draw me across the rocky slopes and into your secret places. Take me closer into you.

Father, I long for your thoughts to be my thoughts and your ways to be my ways. I long to be renewed completely. I long to walk and live in your grace and mercy without interruption. And as I long, you also long. As you draw, I will come. I will step across deep crevices, climb up steep cliffs, walk through tough places, and swim in rough waters as you teach me and train me in your goodness. And I will rejoice again and again in the abundance of your life in me.

Taking Inventory

Whom have I in heaven but You? And I have no delight or desire on earth besides You. My flesh and my heart may fail, but God is the Rock and firm Strength of my heart and my Portion forever.

Psalm 73:25–26 (AMP)

Each New Year's Day is like a beginning, to some degree. It is a time when many are making lists of resolutions and starting over again, usually on things that didn't quite get finished from last year's list. It really is pretty neat to have a time and space when we can take inventory and regroup; seeing where we are along the timeline can be both encouraging and challenging.

But there is so much more to it than just deciding on which habits we'd like to break or form. It's an opportunity to ask, seek, and knock in the high places—a chance to be reminded of what the Spirit has already said, and to hear instruction, direction, and encouragement for the future.

First, let's look at where we've been. The Spirit wants us to remember foundational, life-giving truths we already know; it's amazing how we can almost lose sight of them in the passion of wanting and seeking more of God. Philippians 3:16 (NLT) encourages us to "be sure to obey the truth we have learned already." Take time to savor again those pieces of understanding the Spirit gave you this past year. Pull out the notes and journals and be reminded of the revelations and lessons. Continue on, steadfast and strong in what he has taught you this far.

Second, know that each and every moment offers a chance to gain new insight and walk in unfamiliar land. Life is not stagnant. It is an ever-moving, ever-changing existence.

Maybe you have regrets from this past year. Did you stumble or fall? Did you even sit down and stop? Maybe you pushed aside something God wanted you to learn. It's not too late. He is waiting patiently, full of love and plans beyond all you can imagine.

Grab onto Jeremiah 33:3 (AMP) and don't let go. "Call to Me and I will answer you and show you great and mighty things, fenced in and hidden, which you do not know."

As we move from year to year and season to season, "I pray that your love for each other will overflow more and more, and that you will keep on growing in your knowledge and understanding" (Philippians 1:9, NLT).

Amy Layne Litzelman

Getting New Eyes

For My thoughts are not your thoughts, neither are your ways
My ways, says the Lord. For as the heavens are higher than the
earth, so are My ways higher than your ways and My thoughts
than your thoughts.

Isaiah 55:8–9 (AMP)

I have never been much of an artist. When I took a beginner's drawing class in college, my bottles were pretty uninspiring. I could never seem to get on paper what I saw on the table. Eighteen years later, I learned that there is more than one approach to drawing[2].

Now, the brain is much too complex for me to explain, and there is still much even the experts don't understand, but suffice it to say, each half of our brain handles incoming information differently. The left hemisphere analyzes, counts, marks time, plans step-by-step procedures, verbalizes, and makes rational statements based on logic. Using the right hemisphere, however, we are able to dream, imagine, understand metaphors, create new combinations of ideas, and use intuition; we can see how things exist in space and how parts go together to make up the whole.

Many of us who are not naturally artistic draw from a logical, planned-out mode and our pictures look flat and lifeless. Artists who paint and draw from the creative, intuitive right brain, on the other hand, pull you right into their pictures. It's not so much about how they draw, but how they see.

In Mark 8:17–18 (AMP), Jesus questions the disciples' ability to see beyond the logical, obvious exterior. "Do you not yet discern or understand? ... Having eyes, do you not see?"

If we look at the world around us through earth-bound, analytical vision, it looks pretty flat and bleak. We see the endless, mindless tasks and cycles in which most people exist. It can be very dreary, even depressing. But if we allow the Spirit to bring us in line with his vision—what a difference. Suddenly we see purpose and beauty and life.

I used to look at the snowdrifts in my flower beds and all I could think of was death; my beautiful flowers were all dead. But then the Spirit opened my eyes. Those flowers aren't dead; they're resting. They're getting ready to burst forth even bigger in the spring. And not only that, but they have thrown their seeds all around them to bring up new life.

What do you see? Are you walking in the reality of heaven, or are you stuck in the realm of humanity? Just as Jesus heard the cries of a blind man on the road to Jericho and restored his sight (Luke 18:35–43), so he will hear you. Just cry out. "Jesus, Son of David, have mercy on me!"

Amy Layne Litzelman

Divine Division

See how very much our Father loves us, for he calls us his children, and that is what we are! But the people who belong to this world don't recognize that we are God's children because they don't know him.

1 John 3:1 (NLT)

I love the Word of God. When I read it I feel like I truly "taste and see that the Lord is good" (Psalm 34:8, NIV). And yet, some passages cause me to wrinkle my forehead and echo the words of Jesus's disciples in John 6:60 (NLT), "This is very hard to understand. How can anyone accept it?"

Matthew 10:34–35 (NLT) was one such scripture: "Don't imagine that I came to bring peace to earth! No, I came to bring a sword. I have come to set a man against his father, and a daughter against her mother, and a daughter-in-law against her mother-in-law." How could the Prince of Peace utter these words? How could this be in the same book that again and again speaks of the importance of unity, love, and peace? As I sat and pondered, the Spirit brought me back to a foundation of my faith: *God is good.* Therefore, it is always out of goodness that he says or does anything. With this in mind, I re-examined the scripture.

First, what was uniting the people whom Jesus was planning to divide? Well, everyone was in the same boat, so to speak. They were hopelessly separated from God and overshadowed with sin and guilt. When Jesus came to earth, his purpose was to become a bridge and make a way for humans to step again into intimate relationship with their Father and Maker (Romans 3:23–24). But a bridge gives a choice between two places and the distinct possibility of division and separation.

Jesus knew that his life, death, and resurrection would divide people. Some would believe him to be God's Son, and some would not; some would have faith and become children of God, and some would stay separated from their Creator. In this way they would be set against each other, living for different purposes and passions. Matthew 12:30 (NLT) states clearly, "Anyone who isn't helping me opposes me, and anyone who isn't working with me is actually working against me." Although this division was inevitable, it was not Jesus's final goal. His goal was to give a choice, wanting all to cross the bridge into eternal life and fellowship with the Father. "He does not want anyone to perish, so he is giving more time for everyone to

Amy Layne Litzelman

repent. But the day of the Lord will come as unexpectedly as a thief" (2 Peter 3:9–10, NLT).

History is full of the stories of men who chose to leave foreign lands, wives, children, and poverty to come to America and build a better home. Dividing their families was a sad reality; going ahead to a better place and working toward a glorious reunion was their goal. In the same way, when we step into a relationship with God through Jesus Christ, we not only leave the poverty of sin and death but often place ourselves at odds with friends and family by our decision. However, our goal should be a glorious reunion by sharing with them the love we have found.

Spring Forth

For as [surely as] the earth brings forth its shoots, and as a garden causes what is sown in it to spring forth, so [surely] the Lord God will cause rightness and justice and praise to spring forth before all the nations [through the self-fulfilling power of His word].

Isaiah 61:11 (AMP)

Typically, I start getting seed and gardening catalogs every February. It always seems strange to think about gardening when it is -18° Fahrenheit with five feet of snow lining the end of our driveway. And yet, just a picture of wildflowers or ripe fruit makes me ache for spring.

My aching is for more than just the grass and flowers of this earth, however. It is an ache in the Spirit—an ache for the things of God to spring forth.

I long for revelation of Jesus Christ to burst forth on the earth in even greater measure. "Where there is no vision [no redemptive revelation of God], the people perish" (Proverbs 29:18, AMP).

I long for the truth of God's character—his love, goodness, wisdom, power, and faithfulness—to be spread to every corner. "Truth shall spring forth from the earth, and righteousness shall look down from heaven. Yes, the Lord will give what is good, and our land will yield its increase" (Psalm 85:11–12, AMP).

I await the moment when every living being will worship the Son of God: "For the Scriptures say, As surely as I live, says the Lord, every knee will bend to me, and every tongue will confess allegiance to God" (Romans 14:11, NLT).

Amy Layne Litzelman

I expect and anticipate the time when the body of Christ will fulfill its purpose: "God's purpose was to show his wisdom in all its rich variety to all the rulers and authorities in the heavenly realms" (Ephesians 3:10, NLT).

Oh, sure, things look pretty cold and barren out there, but my faith is bursting with hope in what is unseen. Our God has promised that his word would not go forth void. He has been declaring to us new things which are about to spring forth (Isaiah 42:9). The ground is saturated with seed, and though we know not how they grow, the harvest is unquestionably assured.

Prepare. Get the tools ready now. Clean out the barn. "You heavens above, rain down righteousness; let the clouds shower it down. Let the earth open wide, let salvation spring up, let righteousness grow with it. I, the Lord, have created it" (Isaiah 45:8, NIV).

Transition

I do not consider, brethren, that I have captured and made it my own [yet]; but one thing I do [it is my one aspiration]: forgetting what lies behind and straining forward to what lies ahead, I press on toward the goal to win the [supreme and heavenly] prize to which God in Christ Jesus is calling us upward.

Philippians 3:13–14 (AMP)

Transition: (1) The act or state of passing from one place, condition, or action to another; change. (2) The time, period, or place of such passage.[3]

Along with the masses, I went to see *The Passion of the Christ*.[4] One reality stood out so vividly to me. The whole movie was a picture, a story, of transition. Christ was transitioning from his earthly ministry and body back into his heavenly kingdom and position.

I kept saying to myself, "How could he have gone through this? How? It was too much. He did too much!" And yet he did it "because of the joy he knew would be his afterward" (Hebrews 12:2, NLT). His Father led him to this place—had actually chosen this season for him—and Jesus agreed to walk through to the other side.

God has put before many of us dreams and visions of his glory that exceed all thought or comprehension. He has shown us places of joy and love that take our breath away. And yet a season of transition always stands between where we are and where he wants to take us. Something must be left behind and something gained in order to go on.

Some of us are in the garden, crying out in pain and confusion, "My Father. If it is possible, let this cup of suffering be taken away from me." We don't understand how we can do what he has asked of us. And yet know this: the moment we say with Jesus, "I want your will, not mine," mighty and glorious grace is released for the journey ahead (Matthew 26:39, NLT). Much of the battle is won with these few words.

Some of us are taking our first steps into this passage of change. Some have been moving through for what seems like forever. Some are to the place of clinging to the cross before us, knowing that victory is at hand. Wherever you might be standing right now, remember, "He will take these weak mortal bodies of ours and change them into glorious bodies like his own, using the same mighty power that he will use to conquer everything, everywhere" (Philippians 3:21, NLT).

As Paul prayed in Ephesians 1, I pray for us, also: that we will understand the wonderful future he has promised to us and realize what a rich and glorious inheritance awaits. Press on. Move through. Have faith. Remember the joy that is set before you. "I want to know Christ and experience the mighty power that raised him from the dead. I want to suffer with him, sharing in his death, so that one way or another I will experience the resurrection from the dead" (Philippians 3:10–11, NLT).

Truth versus Fact

And now, O Lord God, You are God, and Your words are truth, and You have promised this good thing to Your servant.

2 Samuel 7:8 (AMP)

I had an interesting conversation with my son Sam when he was about fifteen years old. We talked of the difference between fact and truth. If you look these words up in the dictionary, they mean basically the same thing. But for those who are in Christ Jesus, they become distinctly different.

Facts are all around us as situations and conditions that are reality according to what we know with our five senses. The fact is that we are surrounded by friends, family, or acquaintances who are sick—some whom have even been told they are dying—and others who are hopelessly entangled in addictions and obsessions. The fact is that we have all fallen into temptation and followed the lusts of our flesh, and most of us have been wounded in relationships, some to unimaginable proportions. The fact is that we are surrounded by wars, poverty, and uncertainty.

The fact is that we can pick ourselves and our circumstances apart and find so many things to worry or complain about. This is the reality in which we live. And yet in the midst of this stands truth.

Truth: "When someone becomes a Christian he becomes a brand new person inside. He is not the same any more. A new life has begun" (2 Corinthians 5:17, TLB).

Truth: "He personally carried away our sins in his own body on the cross so that we can be dead to sin and live for what is right. You have been healed by his wounds" (1 Peter 2:24, NLT).

Truth: "But unto you who revere and worshipfully fear My name shall the Sun of Righteousness arise with healing in His wings and His beams, and you shall go forth and gambol like calves [released] from the stall and leap for joy" (Malachi 4:2, AMP).

Truth: "I have told you all this so that you may have peace in me. Here on earth you will have many trials and sorrows. But take heart, because I have overcome the world" (John 16:33 NLT).

Truth: "The Lord upholds all those who fall and lifts up all who are bowed down" (Psalm 145:14, NLT).

Truth: "My enemies will retreat when I call to you for help. This I know: God is on my side" (Psalm 56:9, NIV).

Truth: "The Lord is close to the brokenhearted and saves those who are crushed in spirit" (Psalm 34:18, NIV).

Truth: "I sought the Lord, and he answered me; he delivered me from all my fears" (Psalm 34:4, NIV).

Jesus consistently took the facts that were presented to him and overcame them with the truth of who he is. Dead men were raised. Blind eyes were opened. Demon-controlled people were given freedom. A man walked on water. Unlearned men spoke with the wisdom of God. Adulterous women were given innocence.

"O send out Your light and Your truth, let them lead me; let them bring me to Your holy hill and to Your dwelling" (Psalm 43:3, AMP).

Treasures of Darkness

Who is among you who [reverently] fears the Lord, who obeys the voice of his Servant, yet who walks in darkness and deep trouble and has no shining splendor [in his heart]? Let him rely on, trust in, and be confident in the name of the Lord, and let him lean upon and be supported by his God.

Isaiah 50:10 (AMP)

I get so excited when I re-discover a verse. I was obsessed by one such scripture for a month: "And I will give you the treasures of darkness and hidden riches of secret places, that you may know that it is I, the Lord, the God of Israel, who calls you by your name" (Isaiah 45:3, AMP). I am overwhelmed by the promises these few lines contain.

First, the promise of treasures in the darkness. We do not go through dark nights of the soul[5], as St. John of the Cross called them, for nothing. We enter into these regions to find treasures that they alone hold. Jewels and precious metals are rarely found on the surface but rather are mined deep underground. Likewise, God's treasures are unearthed when we enter, willingly or unwillingly, into dark regions and dig deep within ourselves and within the caverns of who God really is. The Hebrew word for *darkness* in Isaiah 45:3 is *chôshek*, meaning "(lit.) darkness; (fig.) misery, destruction, death, ignorance, sorrow, wickedness: dark(-ness), night, obscurity."[6] What treasures have you discovered in your times of darkness?

Secondly is the promise of hidden riches in secret places. A well-known verse, Jeremiah 33:3 (AMP), says, "Call to Me and I will answer you and show you great and mighty things, fenced in and hidden, which you do not know (do not distinguish and recognize, have knowledge of or understand)." How absolutely mind-boggling that the master architect and creator of the universe, the one who knows tens of thousands of languages, the wisdom beyond all wisdom and power beyond all powers longs to show us his secrets, his riches. He longs to answer our toughest questions and give understanding for our deepest ponderings. He yearns to take us deep into his thoughts, desires, and plans.

This brings me to the most astonishing promise: "that you may know it is I…who calls you by your name." Why does he long to whisper his secrets to us? Why do we endure the darkness to find the treasures? Why? To know the one whose voice we hear deep in the center of our being. To know the one who knows us and calls us by our name. He is the treasure. He is the riches. He is the reason all darkness becomes a well-lighted place.

"Rejoice not against me, O my enemy! When I fall, I shall arise; when I sit in darkness, the Lord shall be a light to me" (Micah 7:8, AMP).

Come up Higher

For behold, those who are far from You shall perish ... But it is good for me to draw near to God; I have put my trust in the Lord God and made Him my refuge, that I may tell of all Your works.

Psalm 73:27–28 (AMP)

One morning the Spirit drew me to stand in front of our breakfast room window. I looked up to the mountaintops before me and heard him whisper, *That's where you're going. Come up higher.* Overwhelmed by the realization that he was calling me to go higher in my spiritual journey, to come closer to him, I was suddenly lost in a moment of awe.

The next morning, again, I was drawn to the window. However, this time a dark cloud hung over and covered the mountain. Thinking of his beckoning the day before, I was reminded of Exodus 20. The children of Israel had experienced the great favor, deliverance, protection, and provision of the Lord. They were now at a pivotal place in their relationship. Until this point, they had always heard God speak through Moses; now God wanted them *each* to hear his voice. But when God came down upon the mountain in a thick cloud, the people heard the thunder, saw the smoke and lightning, and reacted with fear. They stood far off, choosing to continue hearing through Moses instead of drawing near to hear God themselves. That decision changed their future.

As we recall, Moses was unhindered by the sights and sounds and, driven by his desire and relationship with God, ascended the mountain. Meanwhile, the Israelites fell into doubt, unbelief, and, eventually, idolatry.

When God calls you to come closer, what is your response? Do fears of the unknown cause you to hesitate? Do traditions or theologies stand in the way? Is it just easier to hear God speak through someone else's teachings and books? Do you worship through someone else's words?

There are pivotal points in all of our lives—many of them. When we allow fear to keep us from God, fear will then direct our thoughts, actions, and futures. When we settle for hearing God only through someone else, we become very vulnerable to temptation and sin. But it doesn't have to be that way. When you step out in faith, through your fears and toward God, you will, in reality, find a place of great love and safety in that dark cloud surrounding him, a place of lush gardens and deep springs. You will soon find yourself so consumed

Amy Layne Litzelman

by his unearthly attributes that you won't want to be anywhere else. What had only formerly been in your mind, he will write on your heart. Then you can exclaim in wonder with Job, "I had only heard about you before, but now I have seen you with my own eyes" (Job 42:5, NLT).

I urge you, when he beckons—even from a dark cloud—run to him. It is the most satisfying place to be.

Love Covers

And the father said to him, Son, you are always with me, and all that is mine is yours.

Luke 15:31 (AMP)

One of the greatest lessons we can teach our children is the value of relationship. It is easy to see how they can be torn in this area, even as toddlers. Is it more important to get the toy, or to share and keep having fun together? Although this is a simple illustration, each one of us will have to decide how we value the people around us again and again throughout our lives.

Luke 15:11–32 tells the story of a father and his two sons. The younger son took his inheritance, went to a distant land, and wasted it all on wild living. A famine swept over the land and he began to starve. Remembering that even his father's servants had plenty to eat, he decided to ask his father's forgiveness and take a servant's position in his house. Upon his return, however, his father saw him at a distance and ran to embrace him. As the son confessed his sin against his father and heaven, instead of taking a place as a servant, he was given the finest robe, a ring, sandals, and a feast.

Meanwhile, the older brother came in from working the fields and discovered the celebration of his brother's return. His reaction to his father's invitation to join them has always grabbed my attention: "But he replied, All these years I've slaved for you and never once refused to do a single thing you told me to. And in all that time you never gave me even one young goat for a feast with my friends" (Luke 15:29, NLT). In all the years of faithful labor, the older son had become hard. He had lost sight of the riches surrounding him and saw only the work. He had also become callous to the importance of relationship with his father and his brother. Jealousy and contention rose up in his heart.

James 3:16 (AMP) states, "For wherever there is jealousy (envy) and contention (rivalry and selfish ambition), there will also be confusion (unrest, disharmony, rebellion) and all sorts of evil and vile practices." These are not small issues. We are living in a time in history when God has promised to reunite the hearts of fathers and sons—spiritual fathers and sons as well as biological fathers and sons. How are we as the body of Christ going to react to this? If we focus on the labor of our Christianity, we will likely feel the same jealousy as the older brother. After all, who hasn't gotten upset when the work was not evenly divided? But if we are focused, instead, on our Father's love for us, seeing the abundant provision that is *always* available to us, we will rejoice when we can share it with the weary and hungry.

There is work to be done in the kingdom of God, yes, but that should never be our bottom line. "But the end and culmination of all things has now come near ... Above all things have intense and unfailing love for one another, for love covers a multitude of sins [forgives and disregards the offenses of others]" (1 Peter 4:7–8, AMP).

Divine Vulnerability

Even the darkness hides nothing from You, but the night shines
as the day; the darkness and the light are both alike to You.
Psalm 139:12 (AMP)

In a dream I saw a forest with very large trees bordering a vast desert, and a wrought iron fence stood between. There were three distinct groups of people: those who lived and hid in the darkness of the trees; the ones who were making their way across the desert; and those who had stepped through the gate toward the desert but then decided to remain close to the fence in the shadow of the forest.

The forest represented life on this earth without Christ, full of fear and death. The shadows and underbrush hid many secrets and dangers. The gate between the forest and the desert was open for anyone who chose to believe that Jesus is truly God's Son and the only hope for life.

Those who chose to cross the wilderness were driven on by a hunger and thirst to know God more intimately. Although it was often hot and dry, they soon discovered hidden springs and gardens along the way. What had initially appeared to be barren and dead soon took on a beauty and life of its own.

Those who stayed by the fence had stepped out of death and into salvation but were now skeptical of the hot, open desert that lay ahead. It seemed far too vulnerable a place. Interestingly enough, the shadows of the forest gave a false sense of security. They had come to believe that the shade covered and protected them from what they could not understand—even a God they didn't really know—but reality was just the opposite. The shadows were only a delusive retreat.

Amy Layne Litzelman

There is a place of false comfort in Christianity where we can deceive ourselves into thinking that we can hide things from the people around us, and even God, and yet still know him. The Bible says that even darkness hides nothing from God. He knows our every thought and action before they occur. The issue of him knowing our secrets is really not an issue at all. The question is this: Will we step away from our false securities and into a place of honesty and vulnerability to really get to know him?

Ecclesiastes 1:9 tells us that history constantly repeats itself; there is truly nothing new. From the beginning of time God has been calling his people to come away from lies and false comforts to meet with him. Over and over the Old Testament records how he beckoned Israel to step away from foolish notions to walk with him. This is still his desire.

> But I will court her again, and bring her into the wilderness, and speak to her tenderly there. There I will give back her vineyards to her, and transform her Valley of Troubles into a Door of Hope. She will respond to me there, singing with joy as in days long ago in her youth...In that coming day, says the Lord, she will call me 'My Husband' instead of 'My Master'...Then you will lie down in peace and safety, unafraid; and I will bind you to me forever with chains of righteousness and justice and love and mercy. I will betroth you to me in faithfulness and love, and you will really know me then as you never have before.
>
> Hosea 2:14–16; 18b-20 (TLB)

Getting Established

You shall establish yourself in righteousness (rightness, in conformity with God's will and order): you shall be far from even the thought of oppression or destruction, for you shall not fear, and from terror, for it shall not come near you.

Isaiah 54:14 (AMP)

What an amazing thing to see a plant that appears to be growing right out of a rock. It always prompts in me the question, "How? How was it able to grow in such a difficult place?"

Hannah Hurnard's *Hind's Feet on High Places* tells of one such flower. In this classic allegory, the characters are named after their main personality trait, and all of nature comes alive in new ways as God's children are led on a spiritual journey to reach the High Places of his love. The way seems especially difficult for the fearful and crippled Much-Afraid, but as the days progress she learns to find beauty in the midst of trial. On one particularly desolate cliff, she was startled to find a hint of life. With the sun shining down, a graceful but sturdy flower was indeed a thing of great beauty. With a soft laugh the little flower proclaimed, "See now! There is nothing whatever between my Love and my heart, nothing around to distract me from Him... There is no flower in all the world more blessed or more satisfied than I, for I look up to Him as a weaned child and say, 'Whom have I in heaven but thee, and there is none upon earth that I desire but thee.'"[7]

You know, we are righteous only by the sacrificial blood of Jesus—nothing more, nothing less. But in this place of shocking grace, God wants our roots to go deep; he wants us to be *established* in righteousness as a shield against destruction and terror.

The Hebrew word for *establish* in Isaiah 54:14 is *kûwn*, meaning "to be erect; (i.e. to stand perpendicular); (lit.) to establish, fix, prepare, apply; (fig.) appoint, render sure, proper or prosperous." It is also to confirm, direct, fashion, fasten, frame, ordain, perfect, and make ready.[8] This difficult but necessary process doesn't happen in a moment. It can take months, sometimes years. It is not like establishing ourselves in the business of life. We can get pretty far on our own strength in the natural things, but when establishing ourselves in righteousness, our greatest portion is humility. We must first recognize our great need and then choose to receive God's flawless grace and mercy. As he shows himself extravagant in our weakness, our roots will go deeper into his peace, his joy, and his compassion. As he strengthens our faith and resolve while removing the distractions of life, we too will be able to say, "There is none upon earth that I desire but thee."

For each of us, as we go to higher places, I pray in agreement with Paul for our love to abound even more in order to "surely learn to sense what is vital, and approve and prize what is excellent and of real value [recognizing the highest and the best]," that we all may live pure, blameless lives and abound in the fruits of righteousness, to the honor of God (Philippians 1:10, AMP).

Amy Layne Litzelman

A Cloak of Humility

I planted the seed in your hearts, and Apollos watered it, but it was God who made it grow. It's not important who does the planting, or who does the watering. What's important is that God makes the seed grow.

1 Corinthians 3:6–7 (NLT)

It is very exciting to look around and see the fields before us: the Word of God is being spread across the planet like never before. Seeds are being planted, watered, and harvested before our eyes. Reports of healings and deliverance are becoming more common; spirit-revealed teaching and prophecy are in abundance. God is truly pouring out his spirit upon all flesh.

But we are not so different from men and women of old. "The thing that has been—it is what will be again, and that which has been done is that which will be done again; and there is nothing new under the sun" (Ecclesiastes 1:9, AMP). The same temptations and tendencies still exist, as from the beginning, and one such tendency is to focus on and lift up leaders instead of the God behind the leader. Over time, I have come to learn and love how God teaches, empowers, and promotes those who show themselves trustworthy. Promotion can be a tricky thing, however. Suddenly, the gifts that were given to further God's kingdom purposes are in the spotlight. This can lead in one of two directions: either it will point to God and exalt his name, or it will magnify the person holding the gift.

In a dream I saw a figure, invisible except for the beautiful coat she was wearing. She had the ability to fly and was trying to escape from an enemy who just barely missed catching her several times. It seemed she was out of breath from the constant effort. In my dream, I remember thinking, *If she just took that coat off, her enemy wouldn't be able to see her.*

There is a beauty to the gifts and mantles God puts upon his people, but if not properly handled, they become an open door for spiritual attack. God's gifts are not like a flashy new dress, worn to attract attention, but rather a treasure that should be hidden under a cloak of humility. But don't worry. This cloak will not suppress the treasure; it will only magnify the one who gave it.

"And Jesus answered them, the time has come for the Son of Man to be glorified and exalted" (John 12:23, AMP).

Being Clean and Ready

As we know Jesus better, his divine power gives us everything we need for living a godly life. He has called us to receive his own glory and goodness! And by that same mighty power, he has given us all of his rich and wonderful promises. He has promised that you will escape the decadence all around you caused by evil desires and that you will share in his divine nature.

2 Peter 1:3–4 (NLT)

We had the funniest thing happen shortly after we moved into our newly built home. Something was scratching around and squeaking in the woodstove. We figured it was a bird, but we were shocked when seven, soot-covered starlings flew out into my husband's face. After cleaning up the mess, we assumed it was just a fluke. But day after day, for several weeks, we pulled a total of thirty-something starlings from our stove. After awhile it wasn't funny, so I prayed that it would stop. But the next fall it started up again. Well, somewhere in the midst of all of this we had a revelation: the starlings were cleaning our chimney! What looked to be a strange annoyance turned out to be a huge blessing.

As Christians, we are a little like chimneys; we need regular cleanings. We may appear nice and neat on the outside, but everywhere we go, everywhere we look, ungodly sounds and images bombard us. Just as Jesus washed the disciples' feet, we still need to be washed today.

Sometimes God allows little annoyances to fly through our lives to knock the soot out of our chimney, showing us what is hidden deep inside that we may not even know about ourselves. At first we may rebuke these disturbances as demonic attacks. But, hopefully, revelation will come: God wants to cleanse me.

Being washed by the word is a precise but sometimes uncomfortable process. "For the Word of God is full of living power. It is sharper than the sharpest knife, cutting deep into our innermost thoughts and desires. It exposes us for what we really are" (Hebrews 4:12, NLT). But, oh, the rewards. "If you keep yourself pure, you will be a utensil God can use for his purpose. Your life will be clean, and you will be ready for the Master to use you for every good work" (2 Timothy 2:21, NLT). Never doubt the importance of this regular, internal purifying. Jesus rebuked the scribes and Pharisees sharply for being more concerned about external appearances than the condition of their hearts. "Blind Pharisees! First wash the inside of the cup, and then the outside will become clean, too" (Matthew 23:26, NLT).

When things start to annoy or disturb you on the inside, maybe God is just doing a little spring cleaning. Dive into the Word and expect the greater reward in the end.

On Earth as It Is in Heaven

Pray like this: Our Father in heaven, may your Name be honored.
May your Kingdom come soon. May your will be done here on
earth, just as it is in heaven.

Matthew 6:9–10 (NLT)

The Lord's Prayer, as it is usually referred to, has completely captured my heart. Especially the lines, "May your kingdom come soon.
May your will be done here on earth, just as it is in heaven." I can't
escape it. It seems to be in my thoughts and on my lips without
me even realizing it at times. "Come, kingdom of God! Come!" my
spirit cries out, over and over again. Why? Why is this such a pre-
vailing plea?

First of all, what exactly is the kingdom of God or the kingdom
of heaven? Is it some far-off place in the heavens where God lives
and we go to when we die? Is it a physical place that exists on earth?
What does it look like and how do we get there?

From the time of King Saul, God's people have longed for a
kingdom that looked like other kingdoms on earth. Man wanted a
tangible place of ruling and reigning over his enemies—a place of
wealth and success. But is that what God had in mind? When the
nation of Israel asked Samuel to appoint a king so that they would
be like all other nations, God made it clear to Samuel, "They have
not rejected you, but they have rejected Me, that I should not be
King over them" (1 Samuel 8:7, AMP).

Down through the centuries while guiding righteous kings and judging rebellious rulers, our God had a plan for a kingdom far superior to man's ideas, "a kingdom of priests, a holy nation [consecrated, set apart to the worship of God]" (Exodus 19:6, AMP). Although the Israelites chose to look to man for leadership, God had a plan to put a king on the throne to unite him and his people in a new way. God, the Father, began revealing more of his plan when the angel Gabriel announced to Mary that she would give birth to "the Son of the Most High" who would be given the throne of David (Luke 1:31–33). Unlike former kings, however, Jesus—God on earth in a human body—would merge heaven and earth to form a kingdom over which he would rule for eternity.

From the very beginning of his ministry, Jesus spoke constantly about the kingdom of heaven, comparing it to seeds, pearls, treasures, leaven, and dragnets. Unlike most kingdoms, being rich, religious, and influential actually makes it more difficult to enter in. Jesus said we must be as little children, humble and poor in spirit, to enter, and that the kingdom of heaven belongs to those who are persecuted for righteousness's sake.

In God's kingdom the servant is the greatest, the poor are rich, the faithful are rewarded, and those who give away all receive more, but those who try to keep what they have will lose it. Jesus said anyone who puts a hand to the plow and then looks back is not fit for the kingdom of God.

The kingdom of God "is not a matter of what we eat or drink, but of living a life of goodness and peace and joy in the Holy Spirit" (Romans 14:17, NLT). It is also "not just fancy talk; it is living by God's power" (1 Corinthians 4:20, NLT).

The kingdom of God is of such importance that Jesus said to seek it first and foremost, above all other things. He also made this startling statement: "And if your eye causes you to sin, gouge it out. It is better to enter the Kingdom of God half blind than to have two eyes and be thrown into hell, 'where the worm never dies and the fire never goes out'" (Mark 9:47–48, NLT).

Amy Layne Litzelman

Let's go back to the questions we asked earlier, keeping in mind that God's kingdom is full of mysteries that can only be understood by the Spirit showing us. First, what exactly is the kingdom of God? More than anything else, it is the dwelling place of God. It is where his nature and character, his authority and dominion, his will and word rule and reign completely. Is it a place far away where God lives and we go to when we die? Yes, it is. The Word says that the heavens are his throne and the earth his footstool, so we know there is a place where God lives separate from us and this world. Jesus said he was going to prepare a place and would come again to take us there, so we know we will go there someday. But it is so much more...

Is the kingdom of God a physical place on earth? Not exactly. Many people over time have looked only to this physical aspect and have missed it. The Pharisees and religious leaders of Jesus's time were looking for a king to come who would once again lift the nation of Israel to a physical place of reigning over their earthly enemies. Today, many people look to God only as a means of trying to overcome earthly trials and problems. Many see God as a generous banker, handing out wealth and power. Although our Father does bless us physically and financially, his kingdom is so much more...

"One day the Pharisees asked Jesus, When will the Kingdom of God come? Jesus replied, The Kingdom of God isn't ushered in with visible signs. You won't be able to say, Here it is! or It's over there! For the Kingdom of God is among you" (Luke 17:20–21, NLT). The Amplified Bible says, "the Kingdom of God is within you [in your hearts] and among you [surrounding you]." When we submit ourselves to Jesus's authority, believing and trusting that he is the Son of God and that only through him can we be reunited to our heavenly Father, we are born of the Spirit and he takes up residence within us. We become righteous because of Jesus, but this is only the beginning. The Spirit within us begins to stir and teach us. As we allow, he will replace old thoughts and actions with the thoughts and actions of our God. We will learn to hear and recognize the Spirit's voice as he leads and teaches. Over and over, day after day, we will have to choose between the old, earthly ways and the new kingdom ways.

Jesus said, "Not all people who sound religious are really godly. They may refer to me as 'Lord,' but they still won't enter the Kingdom of Heaven. The decisive issue is whether they obey my Father in heaven" (Matthew 7:21, NLT).

Obedience to God's will is vital. This obedience is not one of regret and hesitation, however. It is an obedience of love and anticipation! Jesus was consumed by the voice of his Father; he recognized the eternal life-giving nourishment and pleasure that accompanied his Father's presence and made feeding his physical body pale in comparison. "Jesus said to them, My food (nourishment) is to do the will (pleasure) of Him who sent Me and to accomplish and completely finish His work" (John 4:34, AMP).

What does the kingdom of God look like? It looks like Jesus, who is the exact image of God. Where is it? It is wherever God is reigning, in heaven and on earth. If God is in us and we are obeying his whispers each moment of the day, we are living and moving in the kingdom of God. One day God may say to give, the next he may say to receive. One day he may tell you to go out and do something, the next he may tell you to stay home and be alone with him. Every day looks different because it is a continuous walk with a God who knows all that is ahead and directs us to fulfill his perfect plans around us. When we are doing the will of our Father in heaven, his kingdom is present and operating through us. When we are walking in the kingdom, we are fulfilling our destinies.

When I pray, "Come, kingdom of God! Come, will of God, on earth as it is in heaven!" I am submitting my will and purpose to God's will and purpose. I am praying that God will rule and reign in me completely. But not just in me; I'm praying that every man, woman, and child would desire to do his will as well. As this happens, all other kingdoms will fall and the works of evil will be destroyed. As the kingdom of God comes to earth—in us and through us—the blind will see, the lame will walk, the deaf will hear, and the captives will be set free. As the kingdom of God is preached and lived in fullness, the Bride will be ready for Christ's return.

Be assured, the body of Christ will display the wisdom of God to the principalities and powers in the heavenly sphere. The kingdom of God is at hand.

Marketplace Christians

While the earth remains, seed-time and harvest, cold and heat, summer and winter, and day and night shall not cease.

Genesis 8:22 (AMP)

Amy Layne Litzelman

Our home sits in the middle of what was once a hayfield. Although there are now several houses, I still see plenty of tall, green grass out my windows. Because of the abundant rains, the farmers are cutting several weeks earlier than usual. As I've watched the grasses grow taller and taller, the Spirit has prompted me that a spiritual harvest is also ready around me, and much earlier than expected. It is time to gather in what God has caused to grow.

When we think of harvesting in the spiritual sense, we often envision going to foreign mission fields, or at least having the gift of evangelism rise up within us. We may picture standing on street corners, passing out tracts, and leading strangers in a prayer of salvation. While these are all very legitimate places of harvest, the picture is so much broader. Just as there are many tasks that need to be done during harvest-time on a farm, so it is in the kingdom of God.

On larger farms and ranches, different people are assigned different jobs. Some drive tractors, some drive trucks, and some repair machinery and keep things running smoothly. Some of the crop is kept and stored for personal use while some is shipped off to distant places. Behind the scene, food is being prepared for tired and hungry workers. Everyone gets involved, but in different ways.

In the kingdom of God, there is a strategic necessity to listen to and obey the Holy Spirit. This concept is so very important when it comes to bringing in God's harvest. We must follow our Master's instructions, or we may waste a lot of valuable time trying to do what others are already doing—or even doing something that is not necessary for this season. Where is our place? What is our task? And what field is ready today?

You may be right in the middle of your field and don't even realize it. Maybe you are confused, believing the Spirit is leading you to do something that doesn't seem to fit into the traditional structures or mindsets around you. This is not an encouragement to go off and do something in left field all by yourself, but rather to find that unique, specific place in the kingdom that Christ made you for. God is so huge and so magnificent. He thought of each of us long before we were conceived. Then he began to plant and nurture desires in our hearts even as children. He put people and circumstances into our lives to reveal to us our gifts and talents, our interests and passions. Our Father has focused much time, love, and wisdom on each of us so that all the earth would be filled with his glory. May our eyes and hearts be open to see our position in this season.

Seeds of Life

Still other seed fell on fertile soil. This seed grew and produced a crop one hundred times as much as had been planted. When he had said this, he called out, Anyone who is willing to hear should listen and understand!

Luke 8:8 (NLT)

One summer I noticed more and more hummingbirds in my flower garden. I thought they would only fly in and move on since I don't have hummingbird feeders. Instead they came back again and again, satisfied with the vast selection of flowers. As I watched this, the Spirit began to show me an analogy with the church.

It has become quite accepted to "hang out feeders" in our churches—choosing programs, music, speakers, and even architecture to draw in the crowds. And it works; there are huge megachurches and popular gatherings across the country. The church leadership works hard all week to fill the feeder full of appetizing food, but when many of these people go home, they feel the necessity to always go back to the church building—the feeder—to eat. Contrast this bird-feeder mentality to growing a flower bed that will produce perpetual food, year after year, as well as seed for more plants.

What if, instead of always trying to figure out how to improve the program, the music, the building—the feeder—we would spend our time on improving the dry, rocky, thorny ground of people's hearts before planting seeds of God's Word (Luke 8:4–15)? This means spending time with people outside the church walls: building relationships, breaking down barriers, helping to dig up stones and pull weeds from hurting hearts. Preparing the ground takes love, energy, and perseverance. But then comes the joy of planting the awesome, powerful seeds of God's Word and watching them mature into life-giving, food-producing plants that will feed not only the one in whom they grow but all those they come in contact with. No longer will they be looking constantly to others to be fed, but instead they will feast on God's faithfulness within themselves.

Look around. Do you see the hungry and poor? Love them into becoming a fertile place, ready for the planting of God's Word, and watch the kingdom spring up around you.

Risk-free Living

For I know the plans I have for you, says the Lord. They are plans
for good and not for disaster, to give you a future and a hope.
Jeremiah 29:11 (NLT)

There seems to be an element of risk to almost everything in this
world. When we tell someone a secret, we risk them passing it on.
When we step out on a new idea or venture, there is the risk of failure. When we trust, there is always the risk of disappointment and
hurt. When we own something, we risk losing it. There is always
a chance for victory and a chance for defeat. Everywhere people
are desperately trying to hold on to their possessions, their rights,
their control, their hearts, scared these things will be snatched away
when least expected. This danger is very real for those who have
not put their trust in Jesus. John 10:10 (NLT) states, "The thief's
purpose is to steal and kill and destroy." Peter also exhorts us, "Be
careful! Watch out for attacks from the Devil, your great enemy.
He prowls around like a roaring lion, looking for some victim to
devour" (1 Peter 5:8, NLT).

There is a place, however, where risk does not exist, a place where
worry and fear are not an issue. It is a place where each step taken
is a sure-footed, secure decision. It is in the kingdom of God, in the
presence of the one true God. You can't lose with God. You just can't.

When you give away—even your greatest treasure—you are guaranteed to receive more in return. "If you give, you will receive. Your
gift will return to you in full measure, pressed down, shaken together
to make room for more, and running over" (Luke 6:38, NLT).

When you step out in obedient faith, even when the road looks like it drops off a cliff, his Word will uphold you. "For with God nothing is ever impossible and no word from God shall be without power or impossible of fulfillment" (Luke 1:37, AMP).

And though it may seem at times that the enemy is gaining ground, the future is still secure. When the dust clears, we will be able to say with Paul, "But the Lord stood with me and gave me strength...And he saved me from certain death. Yes, and the Lord will deliver me from every evil attack and will bring me safely to his heavenly Kingdom. To God be the glory forever and ever" (2 Timothy 4:17–18, NLT).

There is absolutely no risk in Jesus. None. His plans for us come from a depth of love, wisdom, and power beyond understanding. What we see with our eyes may appear risky, even hopeless, but his Word declares, "My purpose is to give life in all its fullness" (John 10:10b, NLT).

How many are the chances we take every day? And yet there is one step you can take with a guaranteed ending. Jesus. He came to destroy the works of the enemy, to put us in a safe, secure place, and to lead us by his own hand. Let the Creator take control and experience what you were created for!

> Your mercy and loving-kindness, O Lord, extend to the skies, and Your faithfulness to the clouds. Your righteousness is like the mountains of God, Your judgments are like the great deep. O Lord, You preserve man and beast. How precious is Your steadfast love, O God! The children of men take refuge and put their trust under the shadow of Your wings. They relish and feast on the abundance of Your house; and You cause them to drink of the stream of Your pleasures. For with You is the fountain of life; in Your light do we see light.
>
> Psalm 36:5–9 (AMP)

Unforgettable Wisdom

Now glory be to God! By his mighty power at work within us, he is able to accomplish infinitely more than we would ever dare to ask or hope. May he be given glory in the church and in Christ Jesus forever and ever through endless ages. Amen.

Ephesians 3:20–21 (NLT)

I once had a vision of God playing a game of chess, patiently moving all the many pieces, lining everything up perfectly for what he intended to accomplish. He wasn't anxious or worried, and he had a very specific plan and strategy in mind. Many times over the years, this vision has encouraged me as I pushed to persevere in prayer and worship. I just knew God had a purpose and was working it all out as I submitted to his leading. Only God can see the whole picture, and so I trusted him to make the perfect decisions.

Seasons of waiting with our limited view can be very difficult, however. At times, God opens our spiritual eyes and gives us a bigger look at the board, but even then we are limited in our understanding. We must simply hold on to the truth and faithfulness of who God is, and to the word he has spoken to our spirits. Then, one glorious day, the pieces begin to fall into place. The mysteries and riddles begin to make sense. The perseverance pays off. And the "complicated, many-sided wisdom of God in all its infinite variety and innumerable aspects [is] now made known to the angelic rulers and authorities (principalities and powers) in the heavenly sphere" (Ephesians 3:10, AMP). What an amazing thought. The God of the universe is truly and totally in tune with the big picture. He has always had a purpose and continues to have a purpose: to show the depths of his unfathomable wisdom through his Son and his Church.

I must say that at times God's plan didn't look very wise to me. At times it didn't look like he was doing anything at all. But as I went back to his Word, over and over again I was promised that he had a plan that could not be stopped or hindered. So, as I bowed my life and my will to him, his plan moved forward.

Where are you right now? Are you holding onto the Word of God as waves of doubt or fear rush over you? How about waves of weariness or discouragement? I have felt all of these, and as I cried out for God's grace, he lovingly enabled me to hang on. God's wisdom is unequaled. God's wisdom is unerring. And as we see it unfold before our very eyes, God's wisdom is *unforgettable*.

Amy Layne Litzelman

Humble Enough to Receive

And after you have suffered a little while, the God of all grace [Who imparts all blessing and favor], Who has called you to His [own] eternal glory in Christ Jesus, will Himself complete and make you what you ought to be, establish and ground you securely, and strengthen, and settle you.

1 Peter 5:10 (AMP)

Grace, one of the most spoken of and sung about words in Christianity. It is of such great importance that all but three of the New Testament letters begin and end with the request for God's grace to be upon the reader. Even the very last words of the Bible reflect this desire: "The grace of the Lord Jesus be with you all" (Revelation 22:21, NLT).

God's grace is not a new concept to me. Many times I have seen his favor, blessing, and kindness cover my mistakes, or enable me to do what was far beyond my ability. Many times I have felt his peace, joy, or kindness well up within me when it didn't make sense—when I knew these feelings didn't come from my own emotions. And yet, I can also find myself in a place of desperation, crying out from my depths, "Father, how do I find your grace? God, show me what your grace really means." In this place I know without a doubt that I cannot move forward or function unless God's presence intervenes. I can see the dark waters surging over my head.

One time as I cried out to understand, the Spirit led me to James 4:6 (AMP): "God sets Himself against the proud and haughty, but gives grace [continually] to the lowly (those who are humble enough to receive it)."

You know, it is not until we are naked of his grace for a moment that we truly begin to comprehend the depth of what we had. The line between standing under the mighty shadow of God's blessing and favor and being exposed to the destruction of the enemy is very thin. God's grace is indeed sufficient to get us through any and every situation we encounter, but we must be in a place to receive that sufficiency.

God's grace is constantly flowing from his throne. We can't stop it. It is a part of his very nature. Ephesians 1:7–8 proclaims that we have been saved, delivered, and forgiven by the blood of Jesus because of God's generous and rich grace, which he has lavished upon us. And yet we must choose every minute to be in the place of receiving, walking, and living in that flow. How do we choose? Humility. It isn't enough to assume. It doesn't work to become lazy and take God's grace for granted. We must choose each day to lay

Amy Layne Litzelman

our life down and take up his life, allowing his thoughts, his plans, and his purposes to be manifested in and through us. We must humble ourselves before him, knowing that he is perfect. Then we will stand under the waterfall of his amazing grace!

"Come close to God and He will come close to you…Humble yourselves [feeling very insignificant] in the presence of the Lord, and He will exalt you [He will lift you up and make your lives significant]" (James 4:8, 10, AMP).

Unstoppable Light

And the Light shines on in the darkness, for the darkness has
never overpowered it [put it out or absorbed it or appropriated
it, and is unreceptive to it].

John 1:5 (AMP)

What an amazing promise. What an astonishing hope. The darkness of this world has never overpowered the light of Jehovah. Never.
Through all the seasons of seemingly overwhelming darkness—personally, nationally, globally—there has always been light.

God's light cannot be switched on and off by human hands or
plans; he doesn't have a switch. It cannot be surrounded by the darkness and covertly or quietly absorbed until it no longer exists. It
cannot be stomped out like a random spark from a campfire. In fact,
when darkness resists the greatest, God's light shines the brightest.
It is like trying to pick up a piece of mercury and having it split into
a thousand pieces. It is like trying to plug a hose with your thumb,
only to have the water spray even harder in every direction.

No matter what man does, no matter how far we turn away from
the one true God—the God of Abraham, Isaac, and Jacob—there is
always a remnant burning brightly in the dark.

How do we become a part of this remnant? By allowing the light
of Jesus within our own individual spirits to overtake every closet
and corner of our souls. Although greed, pride, rebellion, fear, or
other debris of our old nature may currently conceal some of his
light in us, it is still there. And it will remain hidden only until we
can stand it no more and bow to him, allowing him to overtake and
remove every fragment of our personal darkness.

God has been separating darkness and light since the beginning of time. His words still reverberate down through the ages: Let there be light. As it radiates forth, his reaction is still the same: "And God saw that the light was good (suitable, pleasant) and He approved it" (Genesis 1:4a, AMP).

As we work, as we play, as we raise our children and plan our futures, may our prayer always be, "O send out Your light and Your truth, let them lead me; let them bring me to Your holy hill and to Your dwelling. Then will I go to the altar of God, to God, my exceeding joy; yes, with the lyre will I praise You, O God, my God" (Psalm 43:3–4, AMP).

Human Life versus Spiritual Life

> Humans can reproduce only human life, but the Holy Spirit gives new life from heaven.
>
> John 3:6 (AMP)

We live in a world where ambition is praised; where a strong work ethic is rare and prized. Examples abound of men and women who started with nothing and worked their way to prosperity. In the natural, physical sense, this is good. The Word encourages us to not be slack, to work as unto the Lord, and to be wise concerning the seasons. We are held accountable for our time and our actions.

There is a place, however, where our good efforts, hard work, planning, and organizing will not get the needed results. There are certain outcomes that can only come about by God, himself. We must simply open the door for him and then step back and watch in awe.

John the Baptist understood this truth. He worked diligently at preparing the way for Jesus; he taught and baptized many. But the time came when John stepped back, acknowledging the uniqueness and supremacy of Jesus. In John 3:26, John's disciples came to him, concerned that "everyone is going over there (*to Jesus*) instead of coming here to us." John, by the wisdom and understanding of the Spirit, replied:

> God in heaven appoints each person's work. You yourselves know how plainly I told you that I am not the Messiah. I am

here to prepare the way for him—that is all. The bride will go where the bridegroom is. A bridegroom's friend rejoices with him. I am the bridegroom's friend, and I am filled with joy at his success. He must become greater and greater, and I must become less and less.

John 3:27–31 (NLT)

There is a phenomenal principle in this scripture. It not only applied to John the Baptist but to each one of us. On this journey with Christ, he gives us tasks to do. Whether they are general commandments found in the Bible, deep internal urgings, or prophetic words spoken personally, God has labor for us to do. God loves our service unto him, but we need to keep our service in proper perspective. No amount of work, knowledge, emotion, or argument will birth someone into the kingdom of God. There is a point where our work can actually hinder God. Humans can only birth human life, not the new life from heaven.

If we only touch people's emotions with our words or songs; if we merely convince them of truth with our knowledge; if we try to heal them with our perseverance and determination, then we fail to give them what they are truly longing for—Christ, himself. Yes, we are called to serve and love others, but it is only the spirit of God giving revelation of Jesus Christ and God the Father that will bring true life, healing, and wholeness.

As the body, we must see the importance of leading others to Jesus and then stepping back and letting him become greater as we become less. Our job is no different than John the Baptist's was: "I am here to prepare the way for him—that is all" (John 3:28b, NLT). Too many times we get so caught up in the work, so caught up in the excitement, so caught up in ourselves that we fail to do the most important part of our work: get out of the way. It is not about us, as much as he adores us and chooses to partner with us in his plans.

Jesus is the way. Jesus is the truth. Jesus is the life. And the only way to truly know Jesus is by the Spirit.

My Determined Purpose

[For my determined purpose is] that I may know Him [that I may progressively become more deeply and intimately acquainted with Him, perceiving and recognizing and understanding the wonders of His Person more strongly and more clearly], and that I may in that same way come to know the power outflowing from His resurrection [which it exerts over believers], and that I may so share His sufferings as to be continually transformed [in spirit into His likeness even] to His death, [in the hope] that if possible I may attain to the [spiritual and moral] resurrection [that lifts me] out from among the dead [even while in the body].

Philippians 3:10–11 (AMP)

We all have goals. We all purpose in our hearts to do specific things, whether we recognize it or not. Sometimes these are well thought-out plans, other times they are rather spontaneous. I want to dig into the intentions of one man—Paul.

First, Paul states in Philippians that his purpose was determined. This implies a set course and a specific goal. Paul was not tossing between the waves of other people's thoughts or opinions. He was not clinging to past mistakes, hurts, or offenses. He had made a determination within himself and would not be detoured by feelings or circumstances. He had tasted, he had seen, and he had experienced something that would leave him unsettled and unsatisfied with anything less.

Within his purpose in Philippians 3:10–11, Paul laid out four specific objectives:

Amy Layne Litzelman

1) "To know him," [Christ, the Anointed One], in a progressively more intimate way. Change is an unavoidable part of life; we cannot stay the same no matter how hard we try. We will either move forward or backward, and Paul determined that the continual, inevitable change in his life would move in the direction of a deeper relationship with Christ, knowing and understanding and recognizing him in a greater way than the days before. He wasn't going to wait for God to search him out and get his attention. He chose each day to run with his Maker, to sit in the quiet of his temple, to step out in faith at his Word, and to trust with joy at whatever circumstances he found himself in for Christ's sake. Paul wasn't waiting for a relationship to happen to him; he chose to be an active participant.

2) "To know the power outflowing from his resurrection." As from the beginning of time, the desire for power is overwhelmingly prevalent today as men and women in every society grapple to get to the top of the pile financially, politically, socially, and even spiritually. Power speaks of possibility. Power brings opportunity. But the power Paul longed to attain is a power that comes through Christ's resurrection— a power that originated in humility, service, obedience, death, and finally resurrection. Are we looking for power in the conventional ways of striving and pushing others aside? Do we want power in order to fulfill our own desires? Or are we willing to serve, let our plans and opinions die, and obey our Father's voice exclusively in order for Christ's power to pour through us unto resurrection life?

3) "That I may so share in his sufferings, as to be continually transformed [in spirit into his likeness even] to his death." As humans, we learn on three levels:

acknowledging information in our minds, receiving revelation by God's Spirit into our spirits, and experiencing it in the reality of our lives. Each one of these levels changes us, increasing in depth respectively. As we look back, probably the deepest, most life-transforming change has come during seasons of suffering while walking out the lessons we had learned in our heads and spirits. Suffering takes us to a point of vulnerability and hunger, which usually wouldn't happen otherwise. Paul was willing, even eager, to suffer in exchange for the joy of being transformed into Christ's likeness. He weighed the cost and saw it as but a small price to pay.

Paul passionately prayed for the Church in Ephesus, "That from his glorious, unlimited resources he will give you mighty inner strength through his Holy Spirit" (Ephesians 3:16, NLT). Why do we need mighty inner strength? So we may be able to endure what is necessary to know the love of our God by experience, not just head knowledge. The journey to knowing God and experiencing his love is a journey full of dark valleys, stormy seas, and dry deserts. It is a journey that requires his strength filling and working in us. We cannot make this trip on our own strength, but as we continue, determined yet surrendered, we will be forever transformed more and more into his likeness.

4) "That if possible I may attain to the [spiritual and moral] resurrection [that lifts me] out from among the dead [even while in the body]." Paul longed to experience God's eternal, abundant life while he was still on earth, while he was still among the spiritually dead. As he determined to die daily for Christ's sake, he anticipated a life full of Christ's character and power. Paul gave up his life and received Christ's

resurrection life. Why is it so important to be rooted deeply in God's love? So we may be filled through all our being with the fullness of God. That we "[may have the richest measure of the divine Presence, and become a body wholly filled and flooded with God Himself]" (Ephesians 3:19, AMP). Paul knew by Jesus's example that being filled with resurrection life would change the world around him. Is this aspiration really possible? Absolutely. It was God's idea first. "Now glory be to God! By his mighty power at work within us, he is able to accomplish infinitely more than we would ever dare to ask or hope" (Ephesians 3:20, NLT).

Many goals are commendable, but may we determine with Paul to separate ourselves from this world and consecrate ourselves to Christ as we reach for the highest reward—God himself.

To the Depths of Passion

And wherever the double river shall go, every living creature which swarms shall live. And there shall be a very great number of fish, because these waters go there that [the waters of the sea] may be healed and made fresh; and everything shall live wherever the river goes.

Ezekiel 47:9 (AMP)

Amy Layne Litzelman

Years ago, I read Jeremiah 20:9 (AMP) and it sparked something in me. "If I say, I will not make mention of [the Lord] or speak any more in His name, in my mind and heart it is as if there were a burning fire shut up in my bones. And I am weary of enduring and holding it in; I cannot [contain it any longer]." I read those words and was struck with the vast distance between my own passion and Jeremiah's. I began to cry out for fire that burns and consumes, even to the marrow of my bones. I did not realize what I was asking for, only that I'd caught a glimpse of something and couldn't look away. This prayer led me down a path, deeper into God's love for me, deeper into my love for him—a journey of revelation and worship.

Although passion, or worship, can never be put neatly into a box or laid out in four simple steps, I want to share a picture the Spirit gave to me from Ezekiel 47:1–12. This is the familiar passage in which Ezekiel saw the river flowing from under the threshold of the house of the Lord. His guide measured out a thousand cubits and the waters were ankle-deep. A thousand more and it reached to his knees. Again, a thousand cubits were measured and Ezekiel passed through waters to his loins. Lastly, a thousand more cubits were measured and, as Ezekiel 47:5 (AMP) records, "It was a river that I could not pass through, for the waters had risen, waters to swim in, a river that could not be passed over or through." Simply put, the waters were over Ezekiel's head; his feet could no longer touch the bottom. From these verses, the Holy Spirit gave me a glimpse of a lifestyle of worship that goes deeper and deeper, with distinct stages or markers.

Our first true encounter with God is like stepping ankle-deep into the river of his presence. While meditating on this, I saw a picture of a young toddler stepping into a wading pool for the first time, his eyes wide with surprise and delight. This beginning stage in our walk with God is marked with a sense of awe. We are both surprised and amazed at our Creator as he opens our eyes to glimpse revelations into the wonder of himself. Just as some children allow fear to take hold and so become afraid of the water, others find it is their favorite place to be. We also make a choice at this stage to either go deeper in the Holy Spirit or to step away.

If we continue, the water soon reaches to our knees and our awe grows into a deep, abiding respect. We are no longer just excited but find ourselves unable to stand before him as we kneel in honor, overcome by his holiness. We openly acknowledge that God is truly worthy of our respect.

As this awe and respect continue to grow, we pass through waters that reach to the waist, a realm of intimacy with our Maker beyond understanding. Suddenly, we find ourselves passionately in love, longing for the tender voice and close touch of our beloved. In this place of intimacy, secret purposes and plans of the Most High are conceived in our innermost parts, plans that will be birthed through our prayers and our lives if we continue to go deeper.

In the fourth level, the water is now over our heads. We can no longer touch bottom and have to make the choice to either turn back where we have more control, or to go on and trust his leading in new ways. Our worship has entered the deep places of obedient faith. We are still in awe of him; we are overcome with respect and love for him; and we are now willing to do anything he asks, trusting completely that he is all good, all wise, and all powerful, even when we can't see the next step and everything around us seems to contradict what we already know. It is here that our worship has the sweetest fragrance and thrills our Lord's heart. Just as the shepherd in Song of Solomon recognized the irrevocable love and loyalty of the Shulamite, at this final depth of worship, our God knows our undivided devotion and trust toward him.

> I have come into my garden, my sister, my [promised] bride; I have gathered my myrrh with my balsam and spice [from your sweet words I have gathered the richest perfumes and spices]. I have eaten my honeycomb with my honey; I have drunk my wine with my milk. Eat, O friends [feast on, O revelers of the palace; you can never make my lover disloyal to me]! Drink, yes, drink abundantly of love, O precious one [for now I know you are mine, irrevocably mine! With His confident words still

thrilling her heart, through the lattice she saw her shepherd turn
away and disappear into the night].

Song of Solomon 5:1 (AMP)

As Ezekiel 47 continues in verses 8–12, the guide explains that this
river from God's throne flows into a sea of putrid water where nothing lives. However, the river pushes death into the outlying swamps
and marshes, turning the sea into a place swarming with life. Fisher-
men shall fill their nets with vast varieties of catch. Trees of all kinds
will grow on the banks, bringing forth their fruit for food and their
leaves for healing.

If we are willing and deliberate in the pursuit of our God, being
led into the depths of him by the Holy Spirit, we will find our passion—our worship—taking us to places we never knew existed.
As we go deeper in awe, respect, intimacy, and obedient faith, we
will see the death of the world around us being pushed back as life
springs forth, life from the very throne of God. "He who believes in
Me [who cleaves to and trusts in and relies on Me] as the Scripture
has said, From his innermost being shall flow [continuously] springs
and rivers of living water" (John 7:38, AMP).

Beyond Sound

And therefore the Lord [earnestly] waits [expecting, looking, and longing] to be gracious to you ... Blessed (happy, fortunate, to be envied) are all those who [earnestly] wait for Him, who expect and look and long for Him [for His victory, His favor, His love, His peace, His joy, and His matchless, unbroken companionship]!

Isaiah 30:18 (AMP)

Through this veil of silence, you beckon me
Through this veil of silence, to the place of dreams
Far off I hear you whisper
Calling deep into my core
Urging, bidding me come
Through this veil of silence

And I worship you

Running hands across the veil, somewhere, somehow
My fingers touch yours and we are one
I am lost in utter darkness
Light so bright it blinds my eyes
But reveals my heart in yours
Reveals your heart in mine

And I worship you
I worship you

No spoken words, only silence
A language beyond sound

Amy Layne Litzelman

Do I Have to Persevere?

[What, what would have become of me] had I not believed that
I would see the Lord's goodness in the land of the living! Wait
and hope for and expect the Lord; be brave and of good courage
and let your heart be stout and enduring. Yes, wait for and hope
for and expect the Lord.

Psalm 27:13–14 (AMP)

My own two sons are now young men, but I had to smile as I visited
with a friend. Her three-year-old son, Daniel, not happy to have to
sit on the toilet, asked a timeless question, "Do I have to persevere,
Mommy?" Although a humorous picture, what a wonderful thing
to see a young mom training her son in this godly attribute, even in
the simple things.

Funk and Wagnalls Standard Desk Dictionary defines *persevere* as
"to persist in any purpose or enterprise; strive in spite of difficulties, etc."[9] This carries with it the idea of enduring in the face of
discouragement, testing, trials, and fatigue. My husband, Matt, once
said, "The only way we can lose is to stop." This statement is so true.
Our hope and our victory in Christ are sure if we only continue the
course to the end. And yet, discouragement seems to be one of our
greatest enemies in the kingdom of God.

Unfortunately, the church has often portrayed life in the kingdom differently than Christ did. He did not water it down or make
it appear rosy. He spoke very candidly:

Whoever does not persevere and carry his own cross and come
after (follow) Me cannot be My disciple. For which of you,
wishing to build a farm building, does not first sit down and

calculate the cost [to see] whether he has sufficient means to finish it? Otherwise, when he has laid the foundation and is unable to complete [the building], all who see it will begin to mock and jeer at him.

Luke 14:27–29 (AMP)

Are we honest with ourselves and each other? Have we really figured the cost of following Christ, each and every step, every day? Although we cannot know all of the specific details of this journey, it is the most expensive walk you will ever take; it will cost everything, up to your very thoughts and intentions. We must be willing to lay down all desire, all control, all of our will, and be molded into the very image of Christ. After determining this is indeed the path you desire, the worst thing you can do is to look back, doubting or wondering if you made the right choice. "Jesus said to him, No one who puts his hand to the plow and looks back [to the things behind] is fit for the Kingdom of God" (Luke 9:62, AMP). Instead, "Let heaven fill your thoughts. Do not think only about things down here on earth" (Colossians 3:2, NLT).

What about joy? Does it always have to be hard? Oh, there is a joy so sweet, but sometimes it is a matter of taking our eyes off the obvious, nagging problems around us and focusing on our Lord. Romans 5:2 (NLT) encourages, "Because of our faith, Christ has brought us into this place of highest privilege where we now stand, and we confidently and joyfully look forward to sharing God's glory." Verses 3–5 go on to say:

We can rejoice, too, when we run into problems and trials, for we know that they are good for us—they help us learn to endure. And endurance develops strength of character in us, and character strengthens our confident expectation of salvation. And this expectation will not disappoint us. For we know how dearly God loves us, because he has given us the Holy Spirit to fill our hearts with his love.

So the very thing—the very trial—that may be discouraging us should in fact encourage us because it is developing Christ's charac-

Amy Layne Litzelman

ter in us. No wonder James declares that our trouble is an opportunity for joy! "So let it grow, for when your endurance is fully developed, you will be strong in character and ready for anything" (James 1:4, NLT).

So, first, understand the goal: to know our Father and the fullness of his love towards us. Second, know the cost: your very life for his. Third, set your sights on the joy of this goal, determining that no matter what it looks like, feels like, or seems like, you will not give up on the prize. Fourth: rejoice! He will be with you through the fire and the flood. There is no place his love cannot reach you. Nothing is impossible to your God, so you are never without help or encouragement.

In the infinitely important days and years ahead, we want to be ready. There is a lot of debate about when the church will leave this earth, but our main concern should be to get ready no matter where we will be. And one of the most important ingredients of being ready is to persevere now. Stand firm in the truth of Christ in you and walk forward in the understanding and peace of the Spirit.

> This is a true saying: If we die with him, we will also live with him. If we endure hardship, we will reign with him. If we deny him, he will deny us. If we are unfaithful, he remains faithful, for he cannot deny himself.
>
> 2 Timothy 2:11–13 (NLT)

Give It Away

Timothy, my dear son, be strong with the special favor God gives you in Christ Jesus. You have heard me teach many things that have been confirmed by many reliable witnesses. Teach these great truths to trustworthy people who are able to pass them on to others.

2 Timothy 2:1–2 (NLT)

Amy Layne Litzelman

I have noticed that something is missing in the body of Christ. Something is terribly wrong. Where are the spiritual mothers and fathers? Where are the mentors who are training up spiritual children? Not just on Sunday mornings and Wednesday nights but in intimate discipleship? I had always hoped to fall into such a relationship, hoping to learn wisdom and truths from an older woman's personal experiences. There is something very precious about a long-term, vulnerable, open relationship with one who has walked the path before and can encourage you through the valleys, warn you of the quicksand, give wisdom for narrow trails, and laugh with you in the high places.

There seem to be three predominant reasons or excuses why older Christians have not stepped into a place of mentoring:

1) They have never reached a place of maturity themselves.
2) They are mature and have many treasures to share but just don't feel qualified.
3) They don't feel that they have the time.

I had a very disturbing dream a few years back. I was in a beautiful, old chapel with dark, rich woodwork. The pastor was standing up at the front, but the pews were empty. I was able to see through the floorboards into the crawlspace below where there were dozens of babies, naked and crying. As I sought the Lord for understanding, he said that this was a picture of most of the church: the leader is acting like all is normal, but the body has never been raised to a place of maturity. In fact, they are like infants needing milk. Furthermore, the reality of this immaturity is being kept hidden, as if it doesn't exist.

Hebrews 5:12 (AMP) speaks of this: "For even though by this time you ought to be teaching others, you actually need someone to teach you over again the very first principles of God's Word. You have come to need milk, not solid food." Chapter 6 continues, "Therefore let us go on and get past the elementary stage in the teachings and doctrine of Christ (the Messiah), advancing steadily toward the completeness and perfection that belong to spiritual maturity."

How? How do we grow up? Although going to meetings and studying on our own can add to our maturity, nothing can replace discipleship—a day-in, day-out relationship full of honesty and learning the Word by walking it out together.

Unfortunately, many who are qualified to be mothers and fathers in the faith don't realize that they are. It is so easy to think someone else is better for the job and knows more than we do. But this is not a reason to hold back the treasures we do have to give. Just as I longed for someone to confide in and give advice to me, there are countless others who long for the same. Have you gone through some valleys and learned the faithfulness and goodness of our God? Have you stepped out on a word from God, watching as he stretched your faith, but then saw his Word hold you up? Have you felt the irrepressible love of God even when you knew your own shame and guilt? Then you have a gift to give someone around you.

But what about the time it takes? How can you fit one more thing into your life? It is a lot like having natural children—life is busy before they come, but somehow it all fits together afterward. Our priorities change, our schedules rearrange, and we come to see that discipleship happens over lunch or in a game of basketball. It happens on hunting trips or while the kids play in the backyard and laundry gets folded. It becomes a part of everyday life.

What is in your hand? What do you have to give away? Someone near you is longing for the treasures you hold.

Amy Layne Litzelman

Beauty beyond Time

Who shall go up into the mountain of the Lord? Or who shall stand in His Holy Place? He who has clean hands and a pure heart, who has not lifted himself up to falsehood or to what is false, nor sworn deceitfully. He shall receive blessing from the Lord and righteousness from the God of his salvation.

Psalm 24:3–5 (AMP)

In a dream, I saw myself going up a mountain trail. I was not alone but with another, walking close, single-file, and yet somehow side by side. It was more beautiful than one can imagine. Sunny. Blue skies. Gray skies. Clouds. Sunrise and sunset. Green grasses. Purple and white and yellow flowers, short and tall. Moss and miniature ferns tucked between the rocks. The path was narrow and flat with loose gravel and rocks on firmly packed dirt. To my right, the mountain. To my left, a steep drop-off.

Before me lay two simultaneous extremes: I walked a dangerous trail; one wrong step and the fall was to inescapable death. And yet the exhilaration and stimulation of the beauty, the ability to see for miles, and the experience of something so unlike anything else up to that point took a hold of our hearts and drew us on. Although there existed a constant awareness for caution and sure-footedness, the beauty far out-weighed the fear. In fact, the fear that lived in the valley below only helped to push us on further up the trail. One wrong step would lead to death and the loss of a chance to experience beauty like we'd only dreamed of. But as we walked sure-footedly, together, on this well-worn path, we would go to heights beyond heights. Together we would see and experience sights, sounds, colors, and shapes never before known at lower places.

This mountain was unique. Over and over we thought we must be at the top because it surely couldn't get any better. But again we would turn a corner to see it rise higher and higher into the sun/Son. And again we would catch our breath and rush forward, cautiously, but with great anticipation and joy. Caution; not fear. Life; not death. Beauty beyond words. Beauty beyond time.

Amy Layne Litzelman

Never-ending Praise

The Lord is my Strength and my Song, and He has become my Salvation; this is my God, and I will praise Him, my father's God, and I will exalt Him.

Exodus 15:2 (AMP)

Do you ever look around and get discouraged, thinking nothing lasts forever? Garbage litters most every corner—garbage that was once something of value and worth. Money is spent in unimaginable amounts every minute for items that will soon be left behind, rusted, rotten, and forgotten.

I remember a special day when the Spirit opened my eyes to see something that *does* last forever. As I sat on our couch and spoke out words of praise and love toward the Lord, I saw each word come from my mouth in a solid, physical form, each word an object flowing from my lips. Then, instead of dissipating into thin air, these words rose up higher and higher, until they entered into the heavens above. There, among the black skies of the universe, traveling in the company of stars, galaxies, and planets, were the words that had only recently left my mouth. They joined millions of other words, circling the universe for all ages.

The Spirit spoke to me that our words of praise, thanksgiving, and worship are not such that they are here one moment and gone the next. We may not hear them after they fade from our lips, but in reality, they never end. Every word of praise we have ever spoken is still being spoken again and again for all of eternity to the glory of God. Every song describing the beauty and love of our King is still reverberating throughout the universe.

I often thought of this vision and the picture it paints, but I had not anticipated experiencing it to yet a deeper degree many years later. I had been leading a worship ministry called Forgiven Worship for three and a half years when the team traveled to Living Waters Ranch in the mountains near Challis, Idaho, to record our second CD, *Unstoppable Love*. After two days of work, we took a night together to concentrate just on exalting God, worshiping with no strings attached and no requests made. We wanted only for our Lord to know and receive our love and devotion. After several hours, we lingered, not wanting to leave this place of rest and beauty. Several wandered back to their rooms while a few of us stayed to record a few more tracks. At one point I went into the restroom and turned on the fan. After only a few seconds I heard what I thought was the

Amy Layne Litzelman

team worshiping loudly in the room outside. It immediately struck me as odd. We were only recording drum tracks, and being one a.m., all other instruments had been put away as everyone wound down in our need to rest. But the music rising over the sound of the fan was unmistakable. I hurried to finish and opened the door to find a completely silent room. At that moment, I knew I had just experienced the reality of the vision I had seen years before. I had heard our praises from hours prior, still praising as they circled the universe, still exalting our God for all of eternity.

Yes, most things in this world do not last. "Here today and gone tomorrow" is an accepted cliché. Yet, one thing will never decay, never depreciate, never wear out, or cease. The praises of our lips are precious treasures to our King, which keep giving unto him for all time.

God's Chosen Dwelling Place

For thus says the high and lofty One—He who inhabits eternity, Whose name is Holy: I dwell in the high and holy place, but with him also who is of a thoroughly penitent and humble spirit, to revive the spirit of the humble and to revive the heart of the thoroughly penitent [bruised with sorrow for sin].

Isaiah 57:15 (AMP)

Amy Layne Litzelman

Ever have those moments or days when you're just hanging on, trying to keep it all together? Your mind is swirling with confusion and frustration, maybe pain or sorrow. Your body wants to react with anger. You're desperately looking for just a small hole in the ice so you can come up for air.

I have definitely had a few of those days. And I know I will have a few more. I used to try to run from them, to try and avoid them, thinking they were my greatest enemy. Over time I learned to embrace these times, seeing them as a doorway to a much deeper place and purpose. In Matthew 5:3–6 (AMP), Jesus sat down on a mountain and began to teach the mysteries of God.

> Blessed (happy, to be envied, and spiritually prosperous—with life-joy and satisfaction in God's favor and salvation, regardless of their outward conditions) are the *poor in spirit* (the humble who rate themselves insignificant), for theirs is the kingdom of heaven!
>
> Blessed and enviably happy (with a happiness produced by the experience of God's favor and especially conditioned by the revelation of His matchless grace) are those who *mourn*, for they shall be comforted!
>
> Blessed (happy, blithesome, joyous, spiritually prosperous—with life-joy and satisfaction in God's favor and salvation, regardless of their outward conditions) are the *meek* (the mild, patient, long-suffering), for they shall inherit the earth!
>
> Blessed and fortunate and happy and spiritually prosperous (in that state in which the born-again child of God enjoys His favor and salvation) are those who *hunger and thirst for righteousness* (uprightness and right standing with God), for they shall be completely satisfied!

Jesus continued on, saying the merciful, pure in heart, peacemakers, and those persecuted for righteousness's sake are also among the blessed and enviable. Does this sound like a top-ten list of things we long for in life? When we think of those whom we envy and want to be like, do Jesus's words come to mind?

First, let me say, I don't go out looking for problems; I don't search pain or sorrow out. But I have come to see the beauty and joy which can and does exist in its midst when we bow before our Creator in love and trust. James 4:8 exhorts us to come close to God and he will come close to us. James 4:6 (NLT) also says, "God opposes the proud but favors the humble." Although James was specifically addressing when we sin and separate ourselves from God's presence, the principles given apply in all situations. Humility is a very valuable commodity to our God. It demonstrates that we know we can't live this life and be his children without him—that his empowerment and love are essential ingredients to our minute-by-minute existence.

On one particular occasion, Forgiven Worship had traveled to lead worship at a conference, but I was walking through a difficult personal situation. My heart was heavy as I asked God how I was going to get up and sing when I was hurting over a misunderstanding with a close friend. I felt empty and drained and clinging to his grace. But as I surrendered to all he wanted to do through this situation, a flood of peace and joy began to rise up in me. It was not only a time of great brokenness in me but also a time of him filling an empty, broken vessel with himself.

Interesting, isn't it? Logic would say to fill vessels with no cracks or holes so they can hold the liquid. But God chooses to fill broken—very broken—pots with himself so that he will spill out on everything around them. Our brokenness is the perfect backdrop for his exquisite beauty and love. It shows him in the perfect light.

The next morning the thought came, *You are exclusively good, God—exclusively good. There is no other person or thing in heaven or on earth that is perfectly good but you. And everything good in us and around us originated and has its source in you. You alone are light and life, and only as we are broken and humble before you can that goodness flow forth and shine in the reality of what it is.*

Living Like an Anableps

Yet it was the will of the Lord to bruise Him; He has put Him to grief and made Him sick. When You and He make His life an offering for sin [and He has risen from the dead, in time to come], He shall see His [spiritual] offspring, He shall prolong His days, and the will and pleasure of the Lord shall prosper in His hand. He shall see [the fruit] of the travail of His soul and be satisfied.

Isaiah 53:10–11a (AMP)

My family lived on a farm in northern Montana from the time I was six years old until I was about nine or ten. We had long, hot summers and long, cold winters. It seemed the seasons came in extremes. I remember my dad, brothers, and visiting cousins coming home, black with soot, after fighting a prairie fire all day. I also remember riding snowmobiles to school when roads were blown in with snow, popping popcorn in the cellar when the electricity was out, and finding a grain bin a mile down the road after a tornado came through the yard.

To the farmers, I imagine the winters seemed terribly slow and the summers very full, as most of life focused on the fall harvest. Although there was always work to be done, the grain bins in every barnyard served as constant reminders of that focus, even in the dead of winter.

One morning while walking, I noticed that I kept alternating my attention between the rocky path in front of me and the distant mountains on the horizon. If I enjoyed the surrounding view a moment too long, I'd find myself tripping; if I kept my eyes on my feet, I missed out on the rising sun. As I thought of this, I realized the importance of seeing both the immediate and the distant. One is not more important than the other, but each can be dangerous on its own.

Think of Jesus. He lived each moment as an act of obedience to his Father. Each thought, word, and action was a willful choice of submission and love. And yet his eyes were always on the horizon—the road to Jerusalem and the return to his Father's side. Focusing solely on one or the other could have brought either discouragement, as he could have become overwhelmed at the surrounding needs and areas of personal surrender, or it could have also caused him to stumble if he only saw what was to come but not how to get there.

I have written several times about dying to ourselves and being broken before the Lord. This lifestyle of surrendered love is God's chosen and perfect plan for us as his children. It is equally important, however, to lift our eyes to the horizon regularly to see the bigger picture and the joy that is set before us. The farthest horizon is, of course, our ultimate reconciliation with the Father at the end of the ages. There are so many more mountains on the horizon before that time, however.

What has God put in your heart? As you have longed for him, what longing has come from him? Do you see the earth filled with his glory, passion and fire poured out through a renewed and purified body? Do you see the spirit of revelation hovering over cities and nations, opening the blind eyes and deaf ears to understand the mysteries of our God?

Jesus lived and walked in the will of the Father, which included bruising, sickness, grief, and death. But death was not the end for Jesus. After offering his life, he rose again to receive three amazing promises: he saw his spiritual offspring; his days were prolonged; and the will and pleasure of the Lord prospered in his hand. In short, he saw the fruit of the travail of his soul and was satisfied. Our walk will include no less if we truly submit and walk the path God has chosen for us—a life of knowing him fully, of sharing in his sufferings so as to be continually transformed in his likeness. Dying daily to our own will and desires does not have to be the end for us.

Amy Layne Litzelman

Jesus set the example; we also are to live the resurrection life, even as we are being broken. Look up. Do you see your spiritual children on the horizon? Do you see a long life filled with the will and pleasure of the Lord? Do you see beyond the travailing of your soul to the sweet satisfaction?

We should be a bit like the anableps, a Caribbean fish. Because of its double retina, it is sometimes called the four-eyed fish. The top retina watches the sky above while the bottom retina watches the water below. We need to be mindful that each step taken is one ordained by our Lord, but we also need to have one eye on the glorious kingdom being built around us.

To Search out a Mystery

The Lord brings the counsel of the nations to nought; He makes the thoughts and plans of the peoples of no effect. The counsel of the Lord stands forever, the thoughts of His heart through all generations.

Psalm 33:10–11 (AMP)

One morning, a few years ago, I walked up on a hillside to pray. There was very large sagebrush all around, and I felt the Spirit lead me to stand between two that were taller than me. As I looked out over the bench to the river below, I was able to see only what was directly in front of me—the sagebrush blocked all vision to either side—and I heard the Spirit say, *These sagebrush represent the doctrines and teachings and revelations given to men. They are good; they will shelter and protect you. But sometimes you need to step out away from them a little, so you can see what is upriver.*

At first glance, this statement may look questionable, even opening the door to heresy and deception. I was a little taken aback myself. It would seem presumptuous to think there are truths beyond what are already established within the knowledge of the church. And yet I long to know my God more each day, so I began to search this out for answers.

First, truth is foundationally important to God, as it should be to us as his children and ambassadors. Proverbs 23:23 (AMP) admonishes us, "Buy the truth and sell it not; not only that, but also get discernment and judgment, instruction and understanding." Truth is the belt that girds and strengthens us (Ephesians 6:14). When speaking to his disciples, Jesus called himself the Truth (John 14:6) and said that the truth will set us free (John 8:32).

The Holy Spirit, also called the Spirit of Truth (John 16:13), was sent to lead us into all truth (John 14:17). We are called to worship in Spirit and in truth (John 4:24) and to serve in sincerity and truth (Joshua 24:14). Therefore, our cry should be the same as David in Psalm 51:6 (AMP), "Behold, You desire truth in the inner being; make me therefore to know wisdom in my inmost heart."

Second, only the sovereign and almighty Jehovah knows and holds *all* truth. "Oh, the depth of the riches and wisdom and knowledge of God! How unfathomable are His judgments (His decisions)! And how untraceable (mysterious, undiscoverable) are His ways (His methods, His plans)" (Romans 11:33, AMP). And yet his plan and desire is to reveal these mysteries, these truths, this wisdom, to his children. "It is the glory of God to conceal a thing, but the glory of kings is to search out a thing" (Proverbs 25:2, AMP).

Our Father God is longing and looking for a people who know and trust him without measure. He is looking for a people who have walked through the fire; who have walked through the flood; who have been tested and tried; and yet have held onto their God to the end. He is looking for a trustworthy bride to whom he can reveal hidden secrets. Does this give us the liberty to step away from the written Word of God to seek new understanding? No, not at all. But I believe that even with all the knowledge and understanding we currently have of the Word of God, personally and corporately, there are still depths of revelation into which we have not yet entered.

Jesus walked in such a place. He often spoke and did things that appeared to contradict the Word, and yet fulfilled it. In like manner, the Spirit may lead us to places that stretch our thinking, but he will only lead us into truth—truth that will always be confirmed in the end by the Spirit and the Word.

Do we want to fulfill the purpose and calling of the church, to make known the complicated and many-sided wisdom of God (Ephesians 3:10)? Do we long for our God to be known and understood for who he truly is? Is it the beat of our heart for him to receive the honor and glory that is unequivocally his? Are we willing to step out from our comfortable understanding and let the Spirit lead us into deeper depths of our God?

Jesus wants to entrust us with the mysteries of the kingdom of God (Mark 4:11). He is looking for a willing, humble, trustworthy, teachable, diligent people who will follow wherever he leads, for his glory. We live in a day when his wish should be our unquestionable aim—whatever the cost.

Not by Might

No unbelief or distrust made him waver (doubtingly question) concerning the promise of God, but he grew strong and was empowered by faith as he gave praise and glory to God, fully satisfied and assured that God was able and mighty to keep His word and to do what He had promised. That is why his faith was credited to him as righteousness (right standing with God).

Romans 4:20–22 (AMP)

I love the way our God thinks. I love the way he does things. It is so unearthly.

Jehovah is a God who calls us to do the impossible, knowing we *can* succeed through his power and wisdom. He speaks mysteries beyond our understanding and then leads us through a journey of revelation. He strips away all of our strength and then pitches a tent of his strength over us. He laughs and dances as we lay all of our desires and ambitions down, knowing this is the beginning of his life within us and the fulfillment of our greatest desire.

Human logic says to look for situations and people who lend themselves to success. Talent, training, strength, and ambition are all taken into account when choosing employees. The odds are considered when placing bets or investing funds. And yet we serve a God who laughs at this logic. He glories in choosing the weak to confound the wise. Romans 4:19 (AMP) states that Abraham's body "was as good as dead because he was about a hundred years old" and his wife, Sarah, was barren. Yet God chose this unlikely couple to become the father and mother of a nation, two people unable to have even one child on their own.

Why would God choose them? Although I cannot presume to know the intricacies of God's thoughts, I see his character so deeply embedded in his choice. Our God looks beyond logic and odds. He looks beyond failures or success. He knows something most of us don't recognize: we are utterly incapable of success, of obedience, of anything good or worthwhile without his intervention. Abraham grasped this. He not only knew his inadequacies but he also knew God's capacity. And in this place of understanding, Abraham "grew strong and was empowered by faith as he gave praise and glory to God, fully satisfied and assured that God was able and mighty to keep His word and to do what he had promised."

Did you catch that? As Abraham gave praise and glory to God, he grew strong and was empowered by faith. Abraham knew he could not accomplish this impossible task, but God could, so he praised God for *his* limitless ability. The result? Abraham's faith in God took him from the realm of impossibilities to possibilities. It moved him from an earthly kingdom into the kingdom of God. It placed him in right standing with God, a righteous vessel before the King. Abraham did not become righteous before God because of something he accomplished. He stepped into righteousness by realizing that he could do nothing, and then believed, trusted in, and relied on the God who is able to do all things. Our righteousness comes in the same manner.

Rejoice! Be strengthened and empowered by faith! Nothing is impossible for our God.

Amy Layne Litzelman

Focus

But John also was baptizing at Aenon near Salim, for there was an abundance of water there, and the people kept coming and being baptized.

John 3:23 (AMP)

Talk about focus—John the Baptist was a focused man. He was driven by one purpose and goal: to point to the Son of God, the Messiah. For several weeks, the Spirit has taken me back to John 3:23, over and over again. Although it appears to be a rather simple and straightforward verse, he began to show me some very profound principles.

The first few readings gave me some general information. Many people were continuing to come to John the Baptist even after Jesus started his ministry, and so he continued to baptize them. To dig deeper, I looked up the names of John's location, knowing this often gives important insight.

Aenon[10] is a place in the valley of Shechem. In the Greek it means "a place of springs." Its Hebrew derivative means "eye, fountain." Salim[11] is a Greek name meaning "to waver, i.e. agitate, rock, topple, (or by implication) destroy; to move or shake." Looking further, I found Shechem[12] to be a Levitical city near Mount Ephraim. Its Greek meaning is "ridge, the neck, between the shoulders, place of burdens, spur of the hill." Ephraim is a Hebrew name meaning "double fruit, fruitfulness."

So, John was at a place of springs—the eye of the land—near Salim (a place of wavering, agitation, and being shaken). This was in the valley of Shechem (a city of priests), near Mount Ephraim (a place of double fruit).

At this point, the Spirit led me to verse 27 of John 3 (AMP), "John answered, A man can receive nothing, [he can claim nothing, he can take unto himself nothing] except as it has been granted him from heaven. [A man must be content to receive the gift which is given him from heaven; there is no other source.]"

Putting all of these pieces together paints a picture of John's focus. John found the eye or center of God's plan for his life and he stayed there, at the place of springs. He didn't waver or get agitated. He did not step to the left or the right of what God had called him to do. He didn't try to be a priest or take on a burden that was not his to carry. He did not get distracted, thinking he could be more fruitful elsewhere. He knew that he could claim nothing and take

Amy Layne Litzelman

nothing to himself but what his Father God had granted him: to ceremonially wash and cleanse people in water to prepare them for a greater one—Jesus.

John was content to do this because his purpose and destiny came from his only source—heaven. He did not stop baptizing just because Jesus had come; he continued as long as there was an abundance of water and the people continued to come. But also, he did not try or want to distract from Jesus's ministering. John knew his season was drawing to an end, and as Jesus must increase, he must decrease. Shortly after this, John the Baptist was imprisoned and beheaded. He finished his race.

What has God called you to? What piece of his plan do you fill? What is your heaven-appointed destiny and purpose? No matter what it is, your heart and focus must be the same as John's: point to the Son of God, the Messiah. Don't waver, don't carry someone else's burden, and don't look for more fruit in another place. Run your race with patient endurance, content that you will gain the prize he is calling you to in Christ Jesus when you finish.

Our Ever-Purposeful God

The steps of a [good] man are directed and established by the Lord when He delights in his way [and He busies Himself with his every step].

Psalm 37:23 (AMP)

One morning I woke to a wonderful surprise: several horses grazing outside my bedroom window. Our neighbor's horses had escaped the pasture, looking for greener grass in our front yard. Although it's not real gentle on the landscape, it was a beautiful sight.

Since the Spirit had spoken to me through horses several times, he had my immediate attention. I watched as they moved on down the road and then took off for my morning hike. When I topped the hill on the other side of the river and looked back, I noticed the neighbors were now working to get the strays back into the pasture. At first I thought they were being awfully lazy in their technique, honestly. One truck crept along, just enough to get the horses running, and then stopped for several minutes. When the horses started to graze, the truck moved a little closer to get them running again—this time in the wrong direction. This process of running them back and forth across a large field by barely doing anything continued for several minutes. Then, quite unexpectedly, the pick-up and an ATV moved in closer and the horses turned and ran through a concealed opening in the fence, back to their home. As I stood there, I asked, "Father, is that how you do it with us? Do you gently keep us run-

Amy Layne Litzelman

ning until we get worn out and decide that the right pasture is the best pasture after all?"

I am amazed as I look at myself and others around me and see how our Father arranges the tiniest little details to get us in the right place at the right time. Sometimes we fight it, arguing that it can't possibly be the right thing, that there must be a better way. But he continues to work in us to change our will and then gives us all we need to do his desires. Sure, there are times when he backs us into a corner and gets aggressive in getting our attention, but if we are honest and think back, there were many, many gentle nudges before the final push. Our God's patience is immeasurable. Look at what Paul wrote in 1 Timothy 1:15–16 (AMP):

> The saying is sure and true and worthy of full and universal acceptance, that Jesus Christ (the Messiah) came into the world to save sinners, of whom I am foremost. But I obtained mercy for the reason that in me, as the foremost [of sinners], Jesus Christ might show forth and display all His perfect longsuffering and patience for an example to [encourage] those who would thereafter believe on Him for [the gaining of] eternal life.

Our ever-purposeful God waited years as Paul (Saul) learned to walk and live every detail of the life of a Pharisee. He gently prodded Paul along, knowing he would stand by at Stephen's stoning, knowing that he would be going down the road to Damascus with intentions to imprison believers of Christ. Jesus knew and waited, knowing the wait would be worthwhile.

Take note of the gentle prodding of the Spirit. Take note of the whispers. Take note before you are backed into a corner, looking desperately for a way out. As we begin to notice how our Father and friend move, soon we will move with him, knowing that his way is the only perfect way. What an amazing God that he would busy himself with our every step.

A Prayer from Philippians

Father, I pray that my love may abound yet more and more, extending to its fullest development in knowledge, understanding, and discernment. I pray that I will display your love in greater depth in my relationships with both you and man so that I may surely learn to sense what is vital and approve and prize what is excellent and of real value.

It is my earnest desire to be untainted and pure, unerring and blameless, so that with a sincere, certain, and unsullied heart, I may approach the day of Christ, not stumbling nor causing others to stumble. Jesus, anointed and glorious one, I pray that I may abound in and be filled with the fruits of righteousness, which come only through you, to the honor and praise of God, my Father, that your glory may be both manifested and recognized (1:9–11).

Father, I am well assured and indeed know that through the prayers of my brothers and sisters in Christ and a bountiful supply of the spirit of Jesus Christ, all this will turn out for my preservation—for the spiritual health and welfare of my own soul and toward the saving work of the gospel (1:19).

I eagerly desire, persistently expect, and eternally hope that I shall not disgrace myself nor be put to shame in anything; but that with the utmost freedom of speech and unfailing courage, now and always, I will magnify and glorify and praise you in this body of mine. May you be boldly exalted in my person—whether through my life or through my death. For me, to live is to have your life in me, Jesus, and to die is to gain the glory of eternity (1:20–21).

Father, I pray for your grace to fill me so that I will not, for a moment, be frightened or intimidated by anything that comes from my opponents and adversaries, for such constancy and fearlessness will be a clear sign, proof, and seal to them of their impending destruction but a sure token and evidence that my deliverance and salvation are from you. (1:28) For I have been granted the privilege, for Christ's sake, not only to believe in, adhere to, rely on, and trust in you but also to suffer on your behalf (1:29).

I choose to work out, cultivate, carry out the goal, and fully complete my own salvation with reverence and awe and trembling (with self-distrust, with serious caution, with tenderness of conscience, being watchful against temptation or anything that may offend you and discredit the name of Christ). I know that this cannot be accomplished by my own strength, for it is your Spirit who, all the while, is effectually at work in me, energizing and creating in me the desire and power to obey you and to do what brings you pleasure, satisfaction, and delight (2:12–13).

I will delight myself in you, my Lord, and continue to rejoice that I am in you (3:1).

I count everything as loss compared to the possession of the priceless privilege, the overwhelming preciousness, the surpassing worth, and supreme advantage of knowing you, Christ Jesus my Lord, and of progressively becoming more deeply and intimately acquainted with you. Nothing is more important to me than perceiving, recognizing, and understanding you more fully and clearly. For your sake, I have lost everything but consider it all to be a ridiculous counterfeit compared to being found and known as in you, not having any self-achieved righteousness that can be called my own (based on my obedience to the Law's demands) but possessing that genuine righteousness that comes only through faith in you, Christ, the anointed one.

My determined purpose is that I may know you [that I may progressively become more deeply and intimately acquainted with you, perceiving and recognizing and understanding the wonders of your person more strongly and more clearly], and that I may in that same way come to know and experience the power out-flowing from your resurrection, which is available to all believers, and that I may so share your sufferings as to be continually transformed in spirit into your likeness even to your death, in the hope that if possible I may attain to the spiritual and moral resurrection that lifts me out from among the dead, even while in the body (3:8–11).

I have not yet attained this ideal, nor am I yet perfect. But this is my one aspiration: forgetting what lies behind and straining forward to what lies ahead, I press on toward the goal to win the supreme and heavenly prize to which you are calling me in Christ Jesus (3:12–14).

Father, I will hold true to what I have already attained and walk and order my life by knowing that Jesus, my Savior, is transforming and fashioning anew this weak, mortal body of my humiliation to conform to and be like his body of glory and majesty. You will accomplish this great task by using the same mighty power that you will use to conquer everything, everywhere (3:16, 21).

I will rejoice always in you, Lord. I will not fret or have anxiety about anything; but in every circumstance, by prayer and with definite requests, with thanksgiving, I will continue to make my needs and desires known—confident that your peace shall be mine. I am assured of my salvation through Christ, and so I fear nothing from you and am content with my earthly conditions, whatever they may be. This peace, which transcends all my understanding, shall garrison and mount guard over my heart and mind in Christ Jesus (4:4, 6–7).

I fix my mind on whatever is true, honorable, just, pure, lovely, kind, gracious, excellent, and worthy of praise (4:8). I fix my mind on you.

No matter if I have plenty or little, I have strength for all things in Christ, who empowers me. I am ready for anything and equal to anything through him who infuses inner strength into me. Thank you, Father, that I am self-sufficient in Christ's sufficiency (4:12–13).

Amy Layne Litzelman

This Place of Our Affliction

The beasts of the field honor Me, the jackals and the ostriches,
because I give waters in the wilderness and rivers in the desert,
to give drink to My people, My chosen, the people I formed for
Myself, that they may set forth My praise [and they shall do it].
Isaiah 43:20–21 (AMP)

For as long as I can remember, Christians have considered being in a dry place a negative thing; a place where we aren't supposed to be and would only admit to with close friends. This is not the impression I get from reading the Bible, however. Not only did Jesus purposefully enter the wilderness on a regular basis but historically, God seems to prefer meeting with man in these desert regions.

Consider when the Israelites came out of Egypt. We usually talk of their time in the wilderness as a time of great misery, as though they were brought through the Red Sea with great victory only to be plunged into a hot land of delusion and disappointment. Was that truly God's perspective? I was reading Isaiah 43:15–21 the other morning and began to piece together a very different picture in my mind.

First, God declares himself to be the Holy One, the Creator of Israel, the King who made a way through the sea and destroyed the horse, army, and mighty warrior in the process. This was a great and mighty act of love and protection from God toward his chosen people. But then he says an interesting thing:

> Do not [earnestly] remember the former things; neither consider the things of old. Behold, I am doing a new thing! Now it springs forth; do you not perceive and know it and will you not give heed to it? I will even make a way in the wilderness and rivers in the desert. The beasts of the field honor Me, the jackals and the ostriches, because I give water in the wilderness and rivers in the desert, to give drink to My people, My chosen, the people I formed for Myself, that they may set forth My praise [and they shall do it].
>
> Isaiah 43:18–21 (AMP)

Why would God so directly want to turn their attention from the miracle of the Red Sea to the wilderness ahead of them? What did this desert hold that was so important after such a sign of his mighty right hand?

First, the Red Sea was a point of demarcation; it was a boundary between the old and the new. Before the sea was a land of bondage and death, the sea itself held the dead remains of their enemy, and the wilderness beyond was a place of freedom and God's provision.

Amy Layne Litzelman

Did you catch that? The wilderness was a place of *freedom* and *provision*. The Israelites may not have seen it that way because it didn't come in the package they expected, but God never left them or forsook them. His protection and provision were constant, though their vision to see and their hearts to believe were weak. Yes, the promised land was important, but I wonder if the wilderness was not even more important. It was the testing ground—the deciding place. It was a place of God revealing himself in a whole new and deeper way. Would his people trust him completely, confident in his goodness, wisdom, and power? Those who believed God to be who he said he was moved on into the promised land; many did not.

Verse 20 amazes me. "The beasts of the field honor Me." The beasts gave honor to the mighty Jehovah for providing water in the desert, and yet most of Israel, the chosen people of God, failed to recognize this astonishing provision.

Do you find yourself in a dry place today? Don't look back toward the land of your bondage, or even to the place where God miraculously saved you from your enemies. Those seasons are over and he is now offering you a great opportunity. He is longing to reveal his sovereignty to you by providing for you in this most hot and dry place. God longs for a people who trust him so much that even when there is no water in sight, we will praise and adore him, knowing that at the right moment, water will spring forth from the sand.

Father, lead us forward. We trust you to feed us with your right hand and bring forth water from the ground. We choose to honor you in this place of our affliction, knowing that someday we will look back on it with deep affection.

To the One I Love

Blessed (happy, fortunate, to be envied) is the man whose strength is in You, in whose heart are the highways to Zion. Passing through the Valley of Weeping (Baca), they make it a place of springs; the early rain also fills [the pools] with blessings. They go from strength to strength [increasing in victorious power]; each of them appears before God in Zion.

Psalm 84:5–7 (AMP)

Far before me a bright light awaits
A darkened night through the sunrise breaks
But down this murky corridor
My weary feet must continue on
An ebony hole between me and the freedom of my soul

But I will walk through this Valley of Weeping
Each tear collects in a pool of refreshing
With each step—growing stronger and stronger
With each breath—increasing in power

Oh my soul, how it yearns for you
I am heartsick for the courts of my Lord
I will contend for just one day
Of your victorious presence and favor
Just to stand inside the threshold
Of my Sun and my Shield—oh my God

Amy Layne Litzelman

Yes, I will walk through this Valley of Weeping
Each tear collects in a pool of refreshing
With each step—growing stronger and stronger
With each breath—increasing in power

I will run on this Highway to Zion
By your sufficient grace
'Til I see your face
No looking back—only straining forward
I am running to the One—the One I love

I am running to the One—the One I love

A Heart Issue

But the Lord said to Samuel, Look not on his appearance or at the height of his stature ... For the Lord sees not as man sees; for man looks on the outward appearance, but the Lord looks on the heart.

1 Samuel 16:7 (AMP)

Amy Layne Litzelman

I love old things. I love driving through the countryside or around small towns and finding old, abandoned houses. Something about them calls to me, making me imagine the laughter and tears, birthdays and everydays, the excitement and boredom that once filled those paint-peeled walls. To many, old neighborhoods and rundown houses only represent disappointment and failure, but to me they are like treasure chests into a past once so full of life. I guess it is true that beauty is in the eyes of the beholder.

It is so easy to see only the outside—the obvious—whether it is with houses or with people. It is simple to focus only on shortcomings and failures. Even when our mistakes are small, they sometimes nag at us like a headache as we play them over and over in our mind. If we had only done this, or hadn't done that.

I remember a couple of days like that. I just kept beating myself up, wondering if I had done the right thing. I felt the Spirit's leading to call a close friend and ask what God had been showing him lately. With a smile I could see even over the phone line, he paused and said, "No matter what error, what failure I make, God's grace is sufficient. In my weakness, his strength is made perfect." Then he paused and sighed. "Isn't that beautiful?" I wept as I realized again the love of my Creator and God. Nothing can separate me from it.

The next morning, as I stood on a benchmark where I often pray, joy and devotion poured from my lips and heart. Then, for a split second, my mind wandered back to that moment of weakness and I thanked God again that he sees my heart first and foremost. As I sometimes slip and slide on this path he has put me on, he knows I'm going to stumble and fall at times. And I think his concern is not so much with my falling as with my choice to get up and persevere to the end. Our Father knows we can live a kingdom life only by the empowerment of his spirit. He knows we will be as Paul at times and "not practice or accomplish what I wish, but do the very thing that I loathe" (Romans 7:15, AMP). Our wise and gracious teacher purposely puts us in situations where we can only stand, make progress, and survive by his loving, powerful hand.

So, this being the case, it only makes sense that he is more concerned with our heart than our flesh. His eyes peer through our outer garment, into our depths, searching the core. What is our deepest desire? What do we groan and ache for as we sit in the dark? Where do our affections lie and what makes our heart leap? Is it to see his glory manifesting in and through us? Is it to see his name exalted and his character made known? Is it to please only him—to obey his every whisper? *This* touches the heart of our Father.

While it is true that we can know a tree by its fruit, and likewise we should be able to see the evidence of the fruit of the Spirit in our lives, there are times and seasons when much is happening on the inside, but the fruit has not yet appeared on the branches. Press on. Desire beyond yourself. Persevere through trials and testing.

> And after you have suffered a little while, the God of all grace [Who imparts all blessing and favor], Who has called you to His [own] eternal glory in Christ Jesus, will Himself complete and make you what you ought to be, establish and ground you securely, and strengthen, and settle you. To Him be the dominion (power, authority, rule) forever and ever. Amen (so be it).
>
> 1 Peter 5:10–11 (AMP)

Amy Layne Litzelman

Power from the Rock

In conclusion, be strong in the Lord [be empowered through your union with Him]; draw your strength from Him [that strength which His boundless might provides].

Ephesians 6:10 (AMP)

On a trip to the mountains of central Idaho, I stood looking at a tree growing from a rock cliff and the Holy Spirit spoke to my heart, *It is going to be very hard when you go home. Very hard. I'm going to make you like that tree, able to grow roots in the rock.* I took a deep breath and prepared myself, as much as I knew to, but growing roots into stone is not an easy thing. Little did I know the course the Holy Spirit would take as he led me into this truth, into God himself.

As I began this journey deeper into my weakness and his strength, I was quickly reminded that humility is essential. As unbearable as the path ahead appeared, I had to choose immediately to submit to it, thereby opening the floodgates of his grace. "God sets himself against the proud but shows favor to the humble" (James 4:6, NLT). Grace enables us to do what is otherwise impossible.

I also began to learn a deeper, more experiential meaning of a few words, as the route would demand:

- Tenacity: to hold fast.[13]
- Perseverance: to persist, to maintain an effort, not to give in.[14]
- Persistence: to continue firmly in a state or action in spite of obstacles or objections; persisting, steady, persevering, lasting; to stand.[15]
- Strength: quality of being strong, ability to endure, power or vigor, to make strong or stronger, to re-enforce.[16]
- Stamina: power of endurance, staying power, vigor.[17]

Now, to walk in these attributes with our own strength is very different than finding a supernatural source in our weakness. The first lasts for a season until our strength is used up. The second starts at the point of our weakness, and so, taps into a sovereign and unending strength. We were not created to be strong because of who we are or what we do. We can only truly be strong because of our union with our Creator, and this only in the realization of our total dependency on him.

Amy Layne Litzelman

As I read Ephesians 6:10 (AMP), suddenly the word *be* stood out. It says, "Be strong in the Lord [be empowered through your union with Him]." It doesn't say to *do* strong, but to *be* strong. Our strength cannot come from our own actions, but from our submission to his strength. In 2 Corinthians 12:9–10, Paul records how he came to know that his weakness was the point of potential God was seeking after to demonstrate his own strength. In fact, it is God's great desire to perfect his strength and power through our seemingly weak and useless bodies. Imagine the joy Paul felt as he realized the freedom he could gain in this place. "Therefore, I will all the more gladly glory in my weaknesses and infirmities, that the strength and power of Christ (the Messiah) may rest (yes, may pitch a tent over and dwell) upon me" (AMP)!

As I read this verse sometime later, I saw a picture in my mind of myself crying out to God, my face to the ground. Then I saw a tent being placed over me. The Spirit asked me, *What do you see?* Well, I could only see the tent; I could not see myself praying inside. The Spirit said, *When you are weak but covered in God's tent of strength, it is his strength that is visible to those around you, not your weakness.* Wow! This was an amazing encouragement for me as I had been wondering how I could ever minister in this weak state. But in our humility, his grace and strength covers us.

Although the process has at times been long and wearisome, I can feel my roots going deeper. I can see his strength increasing. I have tasted the honey from the rock and have been refreshed from the waters that pour forth. I will declare with David, "The Lord lives! Blessed be my rock; and let the God of my salvation be exalted" (Psalm 18:46, AMP).

Beautiful in Its Time

To everything there is a season, and a time for every matter or purpose under heaven: A time to be born and a time to die, a time to plant and a time to pluck up what is planted.

A time to weep and a time to laugh, a time to mourn and a time to dance.

He has made everything beautiful in its time.

Ecclesiastes 3:1–2,4,11a (AMP)

The Word of God is packed full of promises. You can't read a single page without finding them. And if there's one thing I see and know, it is the promise of morning after night, life after death, freedom after captivity, healing after pain, and joy after sorrow. It's everywhere. If we just wait, hope, believe, and trust long enough, the seasons must change. To everything there is a season, and each season *must* give way to the next.

I was reading in Jeremiah and I just couldn't get away from this truth. Everywhere I looked it was jumping off the page:

Thus say the Lord: Restrain your voice from weeping and your eyes from tears, for your work shall be rewarded, says the Lord; and [your children] shall return from the enemy's land. And there is hope for your future, says the Lord; your children shall come back to their own country.

Jeremiah 31:16–17 (AMP)

For thus says the Lord of hosts, the God of Israel: Houses and fields and vineyards shall be purchased yet again in this land.

Amy Layne Litzelman

Alas, Lord God! Behold, You have made the heavens and the earth by Your great power and by Your outstretched arm! There is nothing too hard or too wonderful for You...

Jeremiah 32:15, 17 (AMP)

Behold, [in the future restored Jerusalem] I will lay upon it health and healing, and I will cure them and will reveal to them the abundance of peace (prosperity, security, stability) and truth. And I will cause the captivity of Judah and the captivity of Israel to be reversed and will rebuild them as they were at first.

Jeremiah 33:6–7 (AMP)

[There shall be heard again] the voice of joy and the voice of gladness, the voice of the bridegroom and the voice of the bride, the voices of those who sing as they bring sacrifices of thanksgiving into the house of the Lord, Give praise and thanks to the Lord of hosts, for the Lord is good; for His mercy and kindness and steadfast love endure forever! For I will cause the captivity of the land to be reversed and return to be as it was at first, says the Lord.

Jeremiah 33:11 (AMP)

Since, in his great wisdom and purpose, the Almighty One created both physical and spiritual seasons, my question is this: Do we know what we are overcoming or accomplishing in the current season, before it is forever gone? And second, Will our hearts stay soft and faithful as we anticipate the future so that we can recognize when the season has changed and a new window of opportunity has opened up? Let's face it. There are times when our circumstances seem to drag on forever! Our focus can become muddied and our faith shaky if we don't stay in a place of constant humility and intimacy with the Lord. We can quickly and easily become complacent and miss the opportune moment if we get distracted by circumstances or temptations.

I have often heard the first half of Proverbs 13:12 (AMP) quoted, "Hope deferred makes the heart sick..." The second half holds such promise, however: "But when the desire is fulfilled, it is a tree of life."

I want to dig a little further here. Below are the Hebrew words and definitions for some of the main words in the first half of this verse:

- Hope:[18] *tôwcheleth*, "expectation"
- Deferred:[19] *mâshak*, "to draw (along or out) continue, defer, extend, stretch out"
- Heart:[20] *lêb*, "heart; (fig.)the feelings, the will, and even the intellect"
- Sick:[21] *châlâh*, "a prim. root; prop. to be rubbed or worn; (fig.) to be weak, sick, afflicted; to cause to grieve, to entreat, to make prayer, woman in travail"

The most common understanding of this verse is that when our expectation is delayed, we become physically and emotionally weak and weary; we may even grieve, becoming sick or wounded. Looking at the Hebrew definition of the word *sick*, however, it seems there is a second possibility. When our expectation is delayed, our heart and will should rise up, causing us to pray, entreat our Father, and even travail in the Spirit for a breakthrough. I believe we have a choice, and this can be the difference between our desires being fulfilled unto life and our becoming weak unto death.

God's desire and aim is victory from start to finish. His purpose is never death but always life. We can allow ourselves to get to a place of disappointment and weariness, however, where our very life seems to be draining away. We can lose hope and even entertain thoughts of stopping. At this point it is imperative to run back to the Father, by the righteousness of Christ, and receive grace to persevere. We must stay in the truth of his Word, worshiping at all times, trusting his very nature to bring us into life. Because of Christ, there is always hope of a greater future than what we now experience. There is always the possibility of his character and glory filling us to even greater degrees if we obediently continue this journey of knowing him.

And let us not lose heart and grow weary and faint in acting nobly and doing right, for in due time and at the appointed season we shall reap, if we do not loosen and relax our courage and faint.

Galatians 6:9 (AMP)

Just think of Him who endured from sinners such grievous opposition and bitter hostility against Himself [reckon up and consider it all in comparison with your trials], so that you may not grow weary or exhausted, losing heart and relaxing and fainting in your minds.

Hebrews 12:3 (AMP)

The Completeness of Personality

His intention was the perfecting and the full equipping of the saints (His consecrated people), [that they should do] the work of ministering toward building up Christ's body (the church), [that it might develop] until we all attain oneness in the faith and in the comprehension of the [full and accurate] knowledge of the Son of God, that [we might arrive] at really mature manhood (the completeness of personality which is nothing less than the standard height of Christ's own perfection), the measure of the stature of the fullness of the Christ and the completeness found in Him.

So then, we may no longer be children, tossed [like ships] to and fro between chance gusts of teaching and wavering with every changing wind of doctrine, [the prey of] unscrupulous men, [gamblers engaged] in every shifting form of trickery in inventing errors to mislead.

Ephesians 4:12–14 (AMP)

Somewhere in conversation, my friend's five-year-old daughter said, "There are just no excuses. Not one tiny, little excuse!" How well spoken. Instead, we often give many excuses for our attitudes, behavior, decisions, or failure to make a decision. There are even certain scriptures that seem to pull excuses out of us. For example, 1 Peter 1:15–16 (AMP) says, "But as the One who called you is holy, you yourselves also be holy in all your conduct and manner of living. For it is written, You shall be holy, for I am holy." Doesn't that just mean that we are to *try* to be holy, but not really expect to? We are human after all.

Amy Layne Litzelman

I have always been taught that we do not truly reach the holiness and perfection of Christ until we die. There was always the implied idea that, although we grow and mature, full maturity is only found after our physical death and entrance into eternity. I would like to make another suggestion, based on scriptures I have been reading lately. I'd like to propose that not only can we reach full spiritual maturity here on earth but that this is Jesus's full intention.

Read again Ephesians 4:12–14 (above.) Look at the depth of what the Word says. Jesus's intention was the perfecting and full equipping of the body that it might develop to the point of perfect unity in the faith and in the full and accurate knowledge of the Son of God. He intends that we reach "really mature manhood," which is nothing less than Christ's own perfection. Somehow, the unimaginable is possible—that we, as his body, can reach the "measure of the stature of the fullness of Christ and the completeness found in Him."

Now, before you say, "But that's only after we die," read on. Verse 14 continues, "So then, we may no longer be children, tossed [like ships] to and fro between chance gusts of teaching." We know that we will definitely not be like children and tossed to and fro when we step into the eternal presence of God after death. There will be no chance gusts of teaching in heaven. So there is only one possible meaning that I can see. In order to not be like wavering children here and now, the prey of unscrupulous men inventing errors to mislead, we must reach this mature place of which Jesus speaks.

But... *Jesus was the Son of God. He was perfect!* Yes, but, "although He was a Son, He learned [active, special] obedience through what He suffered" (Hebrews 5:8, AMP).

But... *Jesus had a unique relationship with the Father that I cannot have.* John 17:20–21 (AMP) says otherwise:

> Neither for these alone do I pray [it is not for their sake only that I make this request], but also for all those who will ever come to believe in (trust in, cling to, rely on) Me through their word and teaching, that they all may be one, [just] as You, Father, are in Me and I in You, that they also may be one in Us, so that the world may believe and be convinced that You have sent Me.

But ... this seems so prideful, to suggest that we can even come close to being like Jesus while in these bodies. It may seem prideful, but the author of Hebrews prayed:

> Now may the God of peace ... strengthen (complete, perfect) and make you what you ought to be and equip you with everything good that you may carry out His will; [while He Himself] works in you and accomplishes that which is pleasing in His sight, through Jesus Christ.
>
> Hebrews 13:20–21 (AMP)

It is neither our good intentions nor hard work that perfect us any more than it is our good intentions or hard work that saves us from death. It is Christ at work in us, renewing and changing us as we surrender each detail of our lives, which brings us to maturity in Christ.

I must admit, my first reaction to the idea of my being just like Jesus was to pull back and think that this is such a prideful, boastful thing. And yet, if we have "the completeness of personality which is nothing less than the standard height of Christ's own perfection," there will be no pride in us, as there was none in Christ. It is not prideful to know we are going somewhere that we cannot get to, save for the grace and mercy of our God. We can do nothing to make ourselves holy except to admit that we cannot do it and then obey God's daily Word to us as he changes how we think and act.

Ephesians 3:10 has been the desire of God's heart since day one: to display his unending wisdom through mankind. How can the body of Christ truly display God's infinite wisdom unless we are emptied of all human weakness and filled with the might and glory of God? I believe the only way we can carry out the perfect will of the Father is by being perfected by the Son—perfected now, before we die, so that we can do what Jesus did and even greater things (John 14:12). Only the mighty power and wisdom of God could accomplish this!

No, I am not suggesting that we can all become gods. Not at all. But I am agreeing with God's Word that says God loves us so greatly that:

Even when we were dead (slain) by [our own] shortcomings and trespasses, He made us alive together in fellowship and in union with Christ; [He gave us the very life of Christ Himself, the same new life with which He quickened Him, for] it is by grace (His favor and mercy which you did not deserve) that you are saved (delivered from judgment and made partakers of Christ's salvation).

And He raised us up together with Him and made us sit down together [giving us joint seating with Him] in the heavenly sphere [by virtue of our being] in Christ Jesus (the Messiah, the Anointed One).

He did this that He might clearly demonstrate through the ages to come the immeasurable (limitless, surpassing) riches of His free grace (His unmerited favor) in [His] kindness and goodness of heart toward us in Christ Jesus.

Ephesians 2:5–7 (AMP)

This is all a great mystery, and like Paul,

I do not consider, brethren, that I have captured and made it my own [yet]; but one thing I do [it is my one aspiration]: forgetting what lies behind and straining forward to what lies ahead, I press on toward the goal to win the [supreme and heavenly] prize to which God in Christ Jesus is calling us upward.

Philippians 3:13–14 (AMP)

To Most Glorify Him

Who are these who fly like a cloud, and like doves to their
windows? Surely the isles and distant coastlands shall wait for
and expect Me; and the ships of Tarshish [shall come] first, to
bring your sons from afar, their silver and gold with them, for
the name of the Lord your God, for the Holy One of Israel,
because He has beautified and glorified you.

Isaiah 60:8–9 (AMP)

I want to continue on in the same vein as the last chapter—coming into the completeness of Christ, for his kingdom purposes. I believe we are moving more and more into a day of which Paul wrote. "For all creation is waiting eagerly for that future day when God will reveal who his children really are" (Romans 8:19, NLT).

Again, the most common thought process in the body of Christ is that we will not display the holiness and fullness of Christ until after our physical death and entrance into eternity. I want to propose, however, that God desires to so fill and lead us with his spirit that our true son-ship is evident beyond question while we still walk this earth. It is in this place of openly manifesting his glory that we can most glorify him. By walking in an unprecedented unity with the Father, the church will stun the world and convince them that Jesus is truly the Son of God.

Quite a few years ago I was reading what I consider one of the richest chapters in the Bible, John 17. Jesus's words reveal so much about him, the depth of his love for the church, and the degree of glory and unity that he and the Father desire for us. As I read his prayer in verse one, "Father, the hour has come. Glorify your Son so he can give glory back to you" (NLT), a thought entered my head that shook me. Very clearly I heard, *Amy, begin to pray this prayer.* I jumped inside and immediately called out for the Spirit's direction. Again I heard, *Amy, begin to pray this prayer: Glorify me that I may glorify you.*

This was such a foreign concept to me that I was fearful to even talk with anyone about it. I began to study the Scriptures to see if God ever desired for anyone or anything other than himself to receive glory. Although I am sure I have touched only the surface, I'd like to share what I have discovered.

There are many instances in the Old Testament where God spoke of glorifying his people:

> Behold, you [Israel] shall call nations that you know not, and nations that do not know you shall run to you because of the Lord your God, and of the Holy One of Israel, for He has glorified you.
>
> Isaiah 55:5 (AMP)

Arise [from the depression and prostration in which circumstances have kept you—rise to a new life]! Shine (be radiant with the glory of the Lord), for your light has come, and the glory of the Lord has risen upon you! For behold, darkness shall cover the earth, and dense darkness [all] peoples, but the Lord shall arise upon you [O Jerusalem], and His glory shall be seen on you.

Isaiah 60:1–2 (AMP)

Thus says the Lord: Behold, I will release from captivity the tents of Jacob and have mercy on his dwelling places; the city will be rebuilt on its own [old] moundlike site, and the palace will be dwelt in after its former fashion. Out of them [city and palace] will come songs of thanksgiving and the voices of those who make merry. And I will multiply them, and they will not be few; I will also glorify them, and they will not be small.

Jeremiah 30:18–19 (AMP)

Although these verses speak literally of Israel, Jerusalem, and Jacob, they are also prophetic words spoken over us as children of God. Romans 3:23 (AMP) states that we all start on the same level playing field. "All have sinned and are falling short of the honor and glory which God bestows and receives." Before we are made righteous through faith, we are all falling short of God's glory. But notice—it is a glory that he not only receives but also bestows on others. Before we have faith in Christ, we are not able to give God the glory he deserves *from* us, and we have not yet received the glory he desires to give *to* us.

Jesus also made a remarkable statement in John 17:22–23 (AMP):

I have given to them the glory and honor which You have given Me, that they may be one [even] as We are one: I in them and You in Me, in order that they may become one and perfectly united, that the world may know and [definitely] recognize that You sent Me and that You have loved them [even] as You have love Me.

What an astonishing thought. The One who created the universe with a word (Psalm 33:6), who willingly stripped himself of all privileges and authority to come to earth and sacrifice his life for our sin (Philippians 2:5–7), took the glory he so rightly earned and gave it to those who believe he is the Son of God. Why? Why would he share his glory? So we can become one with the Father just as he and the Father are one—so that we may glorify him in return.

Jesus, as always, gives us the perfect example. He walked in utter and complete submission and obedience to his Father. In this place, they were utterly and completely unified, and all that belonged to the Father belonged to him. For this reason, Jesus was able to glorify his Father so profoundly, by his words and through his actions. When we abandon ourselves to the Holy Spirit's leading, we also become one with our Father. He will begin to tell us his thoughts and desires; he will fill us with his character and power. As we become like him, we will truly honor him. As he fills us with his glory, we will glorify him in return.

I walk and pray often, and many times I find myself prophesying to the land and the animals around me, "It's coming! It's coming! The revelation of the sons of God is coming!" We, as the body of Christ, should so reveal the glory of God that we have nothing in common with earth and everything in common with heaven. When Habakkuk prophesied a coming day when the world would be filled with the knowledge of the glory of the Lord as the waters cover the sea, he was seeing an ocean of God's children who walk the earth demonstrating God's glory.

I long for the fulfillment of Zechariah 8:20–23. I long for the world to be provoked to such hunger and jealousy by our passionate purity that, even when we are not consciously doing or saying anything, the weight of God in us causes them to grab at our garments and say, "Let us go with you, for we have heard that God is with you." The day is coming when those who belong to the Lord of hosts will show forth his glory in such a way that nations will again cry out, "What must I do to be saved?"

With this in view we constantly pray for you, that our God may deem and count you worthy of [your] calling and [His] every gracious purpose of goodness, and with power may complete in [your] every particular work of faith (faith which is that leaning of the whole human personality on God in absolute trust and confidence in His power, wisdom, and goodness).

Thus may the name of our Lord Jesus Christ be glorified and become more glorious through and in you, and may you [also be glorified] in Him according to the grace (favor and blessing) of our God and the Lord Jesus Christ (the Messiah, the Anointed One).

2 Thessalonians 1:11–12 (AMP)

Amy Layne Litzelman

Balancing the Checkbook

And my God will liberally supply (fill to the full) your every
need according to His riches in glory in Christ Jesus. To our
God and Father be glory forever and ever (through the endless
eternities of the eternities). Amen (so be it).
Philippians 4:19–20 (AMP)

While balancing our checkbook with the statement on the com-
puter, I found a couple of errors. At one point we had calculated
incorrectly, adding in our head instead of using a calculator, and
thought we were short of funds. We quickly transferred money from
savings to cover the bills, but we actually had money in our account
all along. Our mistake caused us to believe we were short when
really we had an excess!

I believe this same mistake can be made spiritually. We miscalcu-
late. We add up our circumstances in our mind, figuring it out with
our logic instead of getting the exact truth from the Word. We think
we are running short of what is needed—be it grace, love, strength,
hope, etc. We try to pull in extra from our own resources but later
find when we calculate it against the Word of God, our balance was
much higher than we realized. In Christ, we had an excess of grace,
an excess of love and strength. We had hope all along but didn't
recognize it.

How do we avoid mistakes that wear us out physically and emotionally? Always use the Word of God as your calculator. Don't try to
figure it out in your head. It never adds up right when we do. Never.

His ways are always beyond ours. His thoughts are always above ours. His bank account—and thus, our bank account—always has more in it, physically and spiritually, than we would guess or calculate through our own means. We have all the riches of glory in Christ Jesus. We are moving deeper and deeper into a time and place where we cannot rely on our own thoughts and ways, even for a moment. We have to see from his perspective, from his Word, because in the end, it is his Word that will stand, no matter how it looks.

Amy Layne Litzelman

Nothing Hidden

For there is nothing hidden that shall not be disclosed, nor anything secret that shall not be known and come out into the open.

Luke 8:17 (AMP)

The most common teaching on Luke 8:17 (above) seems to concern the keeping of secrets. Eventually, all we have said, thought, or done in secret will be exposed. And, usually, this is taught in the context of all of our wrongdoing being exposed. While this is a valid and truthful principle, I believe there is much more to what Jesus was saying.

He had just finished sharing the parable of the seeds and the sower to the crowds. Afterward, he privately explained its meaning to the disciples, knowing they had ears to hear and hearts to comprehend. They had been given the privilege of growing in their knowledge and understanding of the mysteries of the kingdom because their hearts were humble and receptive. As Jesus concluded his explanation of the parable, there are several verses that seem to stand alone. However, I believe they are actually linked together for an important picture.

But as for that [seed] in the good soil, these are [the people] who, hearing the Word, hold it fast in a just (noble, virtuous) and worthy heart, and steadily bring forth fruit with patience.

No one after he has lighted a lamp covers it with a vessel or puts it under a [dining table] couch; but he puts it on a lampstand, that those who come in may see the light.

For there is nothing hidden that shall not be disclosed, nor anything secret that shall not be known and come out into the open.

Be careful therefore how you listen. For to him who has [spiritual knowledge] will more be given; and from him who does not have [spiritual knowledge], even what he thinks and guesses and supposes that he has will be taken away.

Luke 8:15–18 (AMP)

This is what I see: Our Father is looking for hearts in which to pour out his Word—just and noble hearts that will receive both the written and spoken Word deeply, allowing it to grow and multiply into a great harvest within themselves and the lives of those around them. Psalm 145:3 states that the greatness of our God is so vast and deep as to be unsearchable, and yet he takes great pleasure in revealing the complexities of his kingdom to his disciples. It is these mysteries and secrets of God's kingdom, I believe, that will not be kept secret or hidden but will be brought out into the open and put on a lampstand for all to see. And it will not be just a few of his secrets. Again, "there is nothing hidden that shall not be disclosed..." I believe God is intent on showing us all things pertaining to the kingdom, if only we will hold them fast to our hearts, steadily and patiently bringing forth fruit.

If you have through intimacy, humility, and hunger received revelation knowledge of the kingdom of God, be encouraged! You can be assured more will be given. But for those who live on the surface, looking only with the physical eyes, allowing doubt and unbelief, temptations and trials, anxieties and pleasures of the world to distract, not only has the word already been stolen from them but the security they think they have in their knowledge will be taken as well.

Oh, Father, may our hearts be found trustworthy, holding fast to your Word with patience. May we ever long for more of the mysteries and secrets of your kingdom, knowing that it is your good pleasure to give them.

Amy Layne Litzelman

To Do Your Will

Then I said, Behold, here I am, coming to do Your will, O God—
[to fulfill] what is written of Me in the volume of the Book.

Hebrews 10:7 (AMP)

This verse in Hebrews 10 just jumped off of the page at me. The author of Hebrews is speaking specifically of Jesus coming to be the single sacrifice for our sins, doing away with the need to offer sacrifices continually year after year. Because Jesus's life, death, and resurrection were prophesied throughout the scriptures, his life was a fulfillment of what was already written of him.

When reading this, however, the thought came to me, *Shouldn't this be my prayer, also?* No, I will not be the single sacrifice for sin that Jesus was, but the Word of God is full of *my* story also. It is full of prophesy about us, the sons and daughters of God, the bride of Christ. Shouldn't our prayer to the Father be, "Behold, here I am, coming to do your will, O God, to fulfill what is written of me in your Word"?

Just think of the connotations. Reading the Bible will take on a whole new depth. We aren't just reading someone else's story. We are reading our story. What's more, it was written by the spirit of God, working through his people centuries ago. God saw you and me from the beginning of time and began to tell our story.

> For we are God's [own] handiwork (His workmanship), recreated in Christ Jesus, [born anew] that we may do those good works which God predestined (planned beforehand) for us [taking paths, which He prepared ahead of time], that we should walk in them [living the good life which He prearranged and made ready for us to live].
>
> Ephesians 2:10 (AMP)

As the body of Christ, we are meant to live according to the mind of Christ, and what better way than to fulfill his Word? Jesus did not pray that we would be taken out of the world, but that we would be protected, purified, and prepared by his Word of truth so as to reveal his glory (John 17). He looked into the future and saw a body of believers who were perfectly united with God and each other, displaying the honor and wisdom of God, so that the world would know he is truly God's Son.

For this reason [seeing the greatness of this plan by which you are built together in Christ], I bow my knees before the Father of our Lord Jesus Christ, for Whom every family in heaven and on earth is named ...

Ephesians 3:14–15 (AMP)

The Beauty of a Dream

Thus says the Lord: Restrain your voice from weeping and your eyes from tears, for your work shall be rewarded, says the Lord; and [your children] shall return from the enemy's land. There is hope for your future, says the Lord; your children shall come back to their own country.

Jeremiah 31:16–17 (AMP)

Amy Layne Litzelman

I read a quote that I just can't get out of my mind:

> The future belongs to those who believe in the beauty of their dreams.
>
> —Eleanor Roosevelt[22]

As children of the one true God, we belong to an assembly of people with the most glorious of dreams. We have a hope and destiny beyond our wildest imagination. The future belongs to us if we only recognize and believe in the beauty of the One who is the author and finisher and in the importance of the role that we play in his plans.

I attended college at the University of Wyoming and would have to drive across vast stretches of high desert to go home for the holidays. I would dread the hours and hours of looking at nothing but dry grass and sagebrush. Then, about twenty years later, I noticed a change in myself. As I looked across those same expanses, my heart felt like it would burst. When I got out and walked the land, I was overwhelmed by what I saw: the miniature wildflowers, the blend of sand and dirt, the varicolored grasses, the soaring hawks, and breathtaking skies. I began to see the tiny details and the bigger picture, both at once, instead of the fuzzy in-between.

There have also been times in my walk as a Christian when I have been in a place of fuzzy in-between. Nothing really stood out. Nothing grabbed my attention. It just seemed like a long, monotonous journey. But as I grew and began to see both the tiny details and the bigger picture, I realized the beauty of a dream God places in our deepest depths:

> And this is his plan: At the right time he will bring everything together under the authority of Christ—everything in heaven and on earth. Furthermore, because of Christ, we have become God's inheritance, for he chose us from the beginning, and all things happen just as he decided long ago.
>
> Ephesians 1:10–11 (NLT)

I know the Father has spoken many promises, and there are plans of reformation and freedom that we, as the body of Christ, have yet to see in fullness. Dreams have been marinating in the hearts of his children for years—dreams that defy every lie and scheme Satan can come up with. I also know the past season of purification and chastisement has left many weary. Some have broken through to new territory, but for many, the breakthrough has not quite come. It's right there in the air, just beyond our fingertips. As the days pass, nagging questions can push into our thoughts:

Lord, did I miss you?

Father, have I sinned or been deceived?

Are you upset at me?

What is going on?

On a vacation to the Oregon coast, I hurried out my first morning to see the ocean I had longed for. I can't explain my passion to be near the waves and hear their roar, but for those who feel the same, you know there are no words. I walked down the unfamiliar road with the sunrise on my back. I knew it was only a mile to the beach; I could hearing the pounding surf and smell the salt air. However, no matter how I followed the winding roads and paths, I could not find my way to the water. At one point I tried to cut through the thick forest but was soon forced to turn back.

I fought frustration as we had come so far and I had waited so long for this moment. It seemed a cruel punishment to be able to hear the ocean but not step into it. I cried out to the Lord, knowing the physical circumstances mirrored the spiritual circumstances in my life. I could hear my Father's heartbeat; I could smell his fragrance. And yet there was a place of fullness and release I was yearning and reaching for that was just beyond my touch. When would I see the fulfillment of the pictures he had placed in my heart and mind?

You know, Job started out very strong. He lost all of his family and belongings in a single day, but he responded by worshiping his God. It was not until time passed on and more and more was stripped away without any apparent response from God that Job began to question what he knew.

But now because God has not [speedily] punished in His anger
and seems to be unaware of the wrong and oppression [of which
a person is guilty], Job uselessly opens his mouth and multiplies
words without knowledge [drawing the worthless conclusion
that the righteous have no more advantage than the wicked].

Job 35:15–16 (AMP)

Even Jeremiah asked questions of God from a place of desperation.
"Why is my pain perpetual and my wound incurable, refusing to
be healed? Will You indeed be to me like a deceitful brook, like
waters that fail and are uncertain" (Jeremiah 15:18, AMP)? The Living
Bible puts it this way, "Your help is as uncertain as a seasonal mountain brook—sometimes a flood, sometimes as dry as a bone." These
shocking words came from a heart desperate to see the fulfillment of
the promises of God, yet now weary in the journey. God's response?

Therefore thus says the Lord [to Jeremiah]: If you return [and
give up this mistaken tone of distrust and despair], then I will
give you again a settled place of quiet and safety, and you will
be My minister; and if you separate the precious from the vile
[cleansing your own heart from unworthy and unwarranted
suspicions concerning God's faithfulness], you shall be My
mouthpiece...

Jeremiah 15:19 (AMP)

We *must* arise in the midst of our circumstances and know that our
God has proven himself worthy of our trust over and over and over
again. We must shake off any residue of the fuzzy in-between and
look again at the bigger picture of his kingdom and the intimate
details of our part. Push through with worship until all you can see
is his face. Know that our God has been longing and yearning from
before the foundation of the world for this generation—for you and
for me—to be made into his image and live a life of consistently
overcoming the enemy. Know that "God is mighty, and yet despises
no one nor regards anything as trivial; He is mighty in power of
understanding and heart" (Job 36:5, AMP).

Let the words of a restored Job rise up within you. "I know that You can do all things, and that no thought or purpose of Yours can be restrained or thwarted" (Job 42:2, AMP).

I made it to the beach soon after my first failed attempt. My initial agony of hearing the waves and not reaching them was soon changed into a joyful anticipation as revelation and thanksgiving welled up within me. The sound of the water was not punishment but encouragement of what lay ahead. Let *this* be an encouragement to you: We too shall soon know our God as he knows us and manifest his glory just as he has told us. We shall see the fullness of his promises at the perfect time.

"For the vision is yet for an appointed time and it hastens to the end [fulfillment]; it will not deceive or disappoint. Though it tarry, wait [earnestly] for it, because it will surely come; it will not be behindhand on its appointed day" (Habakkuk 2:3, AMP).

Without doubt, the future belongs to our God and his own.

Amy Layne Litzelman

Refreshing
Repentance

So repent (change your mind and purpose); turn around and return [to God], that your sins may be erased (blotted out, wiped clean), that times of refreshing (of recovering from the effects of heat, of reviving with fresh air) may come from the presence of the Lord.

Acts 3:19 (AMP)

Ever have those days or seasons when it seems that you are constantly repenting? Does it leave you feeling strengthened or weary? I was praying for a friend who mentioned being in this place and the Spirit reminded me of Acts 3:19. Repentance accomplishes two specific, important things: it erases our sins and it brings us into the presence of our God and Father, where we will be refreshed and encouraged. If you repent and don't feel refreshed, either you are beating yourself up, or you are allowing demonic spirits to beat you up.

I didn't understand for many years what Romans 8:1 (NLT) meant when it said, "So now there is no condemnation for those who belong to Christ Jesus." I had heard this verse over and over, but I just didn't get it until the Spirit gave me understanding. Let me put it this way: Do you ever analyze and replay your faults and mistakes in your mind? Do you go back and ask forgiveness for something that you have already repented? Do you stop short of what you would like to do or accomplish because you feel you are unworthy, even though you have taken your past sins before the cross and asked Jesus for forgiveness? This is condemnation. You have condemned yourself to living under the curse of sin simply by not receiving the forgiveness Jesus has already given to you the first time you went to him.

Repentance is more than being sorry. As Acts 3:19 states, it is changing your mind and purpose; it is turning around and returning to God in an area where you were walking away from him by your actions and thoughts. Repentance comes from having a revelation of the truth of your error and the truth of his mercy and love. And repentance always brings refreshing; it always takes you back into the arms of God. If you don't feel the peace and rest of God's presence, grab onto 1 John 1:9 (AMP):

> If we [freely] admit that we have sinned and confess our sins, He is faithful and just (true to His own nature and promises) and will forgive our sins [dismiss our lawlessness] and [continuously] cleanse us from all unrighteousness [everything not in conformity to His will in purpose, thought, and action].

Refuse to agree with any and every thought that tries to keep you from knowing who Jesus truly is, bringing your thoughts into obedience with his thoughts. Bathe yourself in the truth of his Word until his spirit grounds you in the revelation of how he sees you and how he is changing you into his very own image.

> But whenever a person turns [in repentance] to the Lord, the veil is stripped off and taken away. Now the Lord is the spirit, and where the spirit of the Lord is, there is liberty (emancipation from bondage, freedom). And all of us, as with unveiled face, [because we] continued to behold [in the word of God] as in a mirror the glory of the Lord, are constantly being transfigured into His very own image in ever increasing splendor and from one degree of glory to another; [for this comes] from the Lord [who is] the Spirit.
>
> 2 Corinthians 3:16–18 (AMP)

Repentance is an amazing doorway into God's presence.

Amy Layne Litzelman

A Cause to Hope

The Lord is my portion, says my soul, therefore I hope in him.
The Lord is good to those who wait for him, to the soul who
seeks him.

Lamentations 3:24–25 (NKJV)

I came home one day to find flies buzzing around the kitchen,
attracted to the fresh watermelon rinds in the trash can. My son,
Eli, was frantically trying to kill them all, but as soon as I took the
garbage bag out to the dumpster, the flies no longer had cause to
find their way into the house. Lesson number one on pest control:
take away their food source.

Proverbs 26:2 (AMP) says, "Like a sparrow in her wandering, like
the swallow in her flying, so the causeless curse does not alight."
Sometimes we see issues in our lives but don't recognize the causes
behind them. Take fear, for example. Did you know that fear can
be a direct result of continual disappointments in your life? Disappointment, especially when it has become ingrained into our
thought processes, actually attracts and encourages the spirit of fear.
Disappointment is such a powerful emotion; it draws the life and
hope right out of us. It causes us to pause and sometimes even stop
moving forward toward our destiny. And yet, many people think
disappointment is just a normal part of life.

One day I was walking and pouring my heart out before my
Father, sharing the hurt of being disappointed in the circumstances
I was in. It was as if he gently tapped me on the shoulder and said,
*Amy, disappointment does not exist in my kingdom. If it doesn't work
out like you wanted it to, just know that I have something better than*

you expected. What a change of perspective! Now when I start to feel disappointed, I stop myself and say, "Father, there must be more than I can see. Your ways are perfect." It has been like breathing on the embers of hope and stirring up encouragement within myself. It brings life that can come only through faith.

"But this I call to mind, and therefore I have hope: the steadfast love of the Lord never ceases; his mercies never come to an end; they are new every morning; great is your faithfulness" (Lamentations 3:21–23, ESV).

Amy Layne Litzelman

Compelled to Victory

But thanks be to God, Who gives us the victory [making us conquerors] through our Lord Jesus Christ. Therefore, my beloved brethren, be firm (steadfast), immovable, always abounding in the work of the Lord [always being superior, excelling, doing more than enough in the service of the Lord], knowing and being continually aware that your labor in the Lord is not futile [it is never wasted or to no purpose].

1 Corinthians 15:57–58 (AMP)

Revival and *reformation* have become such familiar words in the church in recent years. Sometimes, when words become too familiar, they lose their impact. What exactly do we mean when we pray for revival? What does reformation really look like? I have been reading *A River of Grace—A Story of John Calvin* with my sons. One story in particular left me speechless. I would like to submit this as an example of what we should expect to happen through us as we become the bride Christ intends for us to be.

As background, the Catholic Church at this time had descended into a pit of manipulation and control by greedy leaders, keeping common men in the dark by not allowing them to read or study the Bible for themselves. Spiritual life consisted of traditions and laws, which kept men in guilt and bondage. Any convictions against the regulations of the church were quickly punished, many times with death.

Around 1540, John Calvin and William Farel were part of a large gathering of Catholic and Protestant leaders. This debate would determine the fate of Lausanne, Switzerland—whether this city would follow the traditions of the Catholic Church, or release the

Word of God to all men and teach salvation by grace through faith in Christ.

On the fourth day of the debate, a Catholic scholar by the name of Mimard declared that the Reformers were teaching the Lord's Supper in a way that went against the Bible and the early church father, Augustine. Although he had remained silent, letting Farel defend the truths of the Bible the first three days, John Calvin now rose slowly to his feet to speak for the Reformers.

> John began to quote large sections of Augustine's writings from memory. The audience stopped their whisperings. In amazed silence they hung on John's every word. He not only quoted from Augustine, but from other early church leaders. He also quoted from the Bible.
>
> He turned to his audience. All shyness disappeared. "Judge for yourselves whether we are hostile to the Bible and the church fathers who knew it so well...We confess our faith based on Holy Scriptures, without any additions from human wisdom."
>
> As John sat down, the audience remained in stunned silence. The learned priests exchanged worried glances. None of them could attack John Calvin's words. He knew too much.
>
> Suddenly, a Franciscan friar stood up. The people recognized him at once as Jean Tandy, one of the most outspoken opponents to the "New Faith." Today he was not the self-assured preacher who eloquently persuaded his congregation to stay with Mother Church. "My friends," he began in a voice choked with emotion. "It is a sin to stubbornly rebel against the clear truth. I confess that I am guilty, because I have ignorantly lived in error and taught you lies. I ask God's forgiveness for everything I have wrongly taught, and I ask you to forgive me, too. I hereby defrock myself so that I may follow Christ and the truth of the Bible alone."
>
> The audience was in an uproar. Within twenty-four hours, all the houses of sin had been closed in Lausanne. In the next few months, a growing number of the clergy converted to the "New Faith." Mimard, himself, became a Christian. When the time came for the citizens to vote, they overwhelmingly chose to become a Reformed city.[23]

Amy Layne Litzelman

How did this 180-degree turn-about come to an entire city? What so captured the hearts of the people that they were stunned into silence and compelled to change? For weeks, months, and years before, men and women gave their lives and hearts completely to the truth, allowing God to do whatever it took in them so as to reveal his presence through them. They endured hardships and persecutions, watching friends and family being put to death because of a passion for their Savior and king. As a result, his glory poured forth from them, leaving on-lookers hungry and thirsty for nothing less than the reality of God's spirit and truth. They spoke words refined in the fire of God.

Again, we are in a time and place where many have laid their lives down before God's throne in passion and honesty, seeking only the truth and the Spirit. And again we are beginning to see opponents of the gospel stunned into silence, leaving all to follow Christ.

Your heart of devotion and obedience is not in vain. Who knows but God how many people have come near to you and were forever changed simply by the fragrance of his love in you? Who knows but God if he will put you before kings and leaders to speak the truth, redirecting the future of nations? Who knows when that small crack in the dam of our enemy's plans will give way and God's glory will truly cover the earth as the sea? Do not become distracted or discouraged by the death around you. Death must always give way when the life of Christ enters the picture.

Just as Jesus encouraged Martha moments before raising her brother, Lazarus, from the dead, let his words now encourage you, "Did I not tell you and promise you that if you would believe and rely on Me, you would see the glory of God" (John 11:40, AMP)? No one keeps a promise better than our God.

But to Maintain a Soft Heart

Lord, my heart is not haughty, nor my eyes lofty; neither do I exercise myself in matters too great or in things too wonderful for me. Surely I have calmed and quieted my soul; like a weaned child with his mother, like a weaned child is my soul within me [ceased from fretting].

Psalm 131:1–2 (AMP)

Amy Layne Litzelman

One of the most crucial and yet difficult attributes to maintain is a soft heart. A tender heart is an invitation to the fullness and completion of God's kingdom in your life; it is the doorway to heaven's possibilities. On the contrary, the prideful or fearful hardening of heart causes blindness and jealousy leading to death.

I'm going to say something here with great caution: following spiritual traditions and practices—including prayer, Bible study, church attendance, and even ministry or service to others—is not enough to maintain a soft heart. It requires more than discipline or habit. A soft heart comes to the one who waits quietly before the Father, submitting to the oil of the Spirit, the removal of sins and offenses, and the exchange of old nature for new.

Jesus was grieved over and over by the hardened hearts he saw around him, especially in those who should have recognized and received him. In Mark 3:1–6, Jesus encountered a man with a withered hand and a group of Pharisees. Anyone with any sense of compassion would have looked upon the crippled man and longed for his healing; Jesus took it one step further. He stepped on the toes of the Pharisees and their rules, speaking life into the dead limb. The religious leaders responded by holding a meeting to discuss how to put Jesus to death over a man being healed! How very blind they had become; how very hard were their hearts. They chose to walk away from the very source of life, even seeking to condemn everyone to death by contriving to take Jesus's life. In contrast we see Jesus's tender heart crying out for God's mercy on those who mocked and tormented him as he hung dying on the cross. What was the difference? What causes one man to walk in humble compassion while another lives in passionate deceit?

Having walked through some very difficult and painful circumstances, I can understand the tendency to try to protect our hearts from further pain or injury. At times, when the road has been long and the journey strenuous, weariness pulls at us and distorts our vision. I wonder if many of the religious leaders of that day had not started out as hungry, passionate young men, full of the prophetic words of God, longing to see his plan on earth. But when things didn't come about as they had pictured in their minds, routine took over and soon passion turned into tradition. Then Jesus walks into the picture, the kingdom of God pouring out in his every word, and instead of being excited to see what they had long hoped for, jealousy rose up against this common man who dared to be different, who dared to be one with the Father.

Think of the elder brother in the story of the prodigal son. He had been faithful in his service to the father while his younger brother had been foolish. Then, at the sight of his brother's humble return and his father's intense forgiveness, a seed of jealousy fell on his heart. What should have been a joyful reunion between brothers turned into blind death for the older son. Offense rose up in his heart against both his brother and his father. Again, I want to point out that faithful service did not keep his heart soft. Reading and memorizing the scriptures did not keep the Jewish leaders' hearts supple. Psalm 119:165 (AMP) says, "Great peace have they who love Your law; nothing shall offend them or make them stumble." It takes more than knowledge of the Word; we must be consumed with a *love* for the Word. We must hungrily grasp at both the sweetness and bitterness of it. As Proverbs 27:7 (AMP) reminds us, "To the hungry soul every bitter thing is sweet."

If anyone had reason to be disheartened or weary, it was David. As a young shepherd boy, he was anointed by the prophet Samuel as God's chosen king, and yet found himself many years later still under the authority and jealousy of King Saul. How he must have wrestled in his mind with the contradiction of this. 1 Samuel 24 records how, once again, Saul sought David's life. God's favor and protection were upon David, however, and he escaped, but not before he cut off a piece of the sleeping king's robe. Look at David's response: "Afterward, David's heart smote him because he had cut off Saul's skirt. He said to his men, The Lord forbid that I should do this to my master, the Lord's anointed, to put my hand out against him, when he is the anointed of the Lord" (1 Samuel 24:5–6, AMP).

From an earthly perspective, David had every reason to harden his heart against Saul, and yet we see here deep remorse at even dishonoring Saul by cutting his robe. Only a soft heart would be smote by this choice. David was one who earnestly sought God's heart—who jealously guarded God's words—and this alone kept his heart tender. And true to his promised word, on the appointed day and hour, God placed David on the throne.

I know of no one who lacks dreams and visions from the Lord, even those who do not recognize them as such. God has placed in the heart of each man, woman, and child desires with roots in heaven. The question is whether we let the journey of life prepare us for our destiny and the unfolding of God's kingdom purpose, or let weariness, routine, pride, and jealousy find ground to grow and what we once strained to grasp be the very thing we stand against?

Francis Frangipane said it well in *The Three Battlegrounds*, "The greatest defense we can have against the devil is to maintain an honest heart before God."[24] An honest heart is a soft heart. An honest heart cries out in pain to the Father but submits under the gentle surgery of his spirit. An honest heart before God is one who will see the kingdom.

The Measure of God's Favor

> I have given to them the glory and honor which You have given
> Me, that they may be one [even] as We are one: I in them and
> You in Me, in order that they may become one and perfectly
> united, that the world may know and [definitely] recognize that
> You sent Me and that You have loved them [even] as You have
> loved Me.
>
> John 17:22–23 (AMP)

In the Old Testament, physical riches and status served as a mark to
distinguish God's people from all other peoples of the earth. Abraham, Isaac, Jacob, Joseph, Job, David, Solomon—the list is evident.
These men possessed great land and livestock. They overcame and
defeated strong rivals. As their hearts sought after and obeyed God,
physical wealth, blessing, and victory were poured upon them.

I want to contrast this to the New Testament and present-day
disciple. So many people in the church are still looking for physical
riches and status to somehow mark them as having the favor of God
on their lives. But is this how God marks his people under the new
covenant in Jesus? What distinguished the apostles and early disciples of Christ? They were not necessarily wealthy. They were not
held in high esteem by much of society. Most were common men
and women who suffered great loss and persecution, and yet they
stood out like beacons to those who were looking. Why?

Jesus spoke to his disciples as he knew the hour was at hand for
his death:

I am telling you nothing but the truth when I say it is profitable (good, expedient, advantageous) for you that I go away. Because if I do not go away, the Comforter (Counselor, Helper, Advocate, Intercessor, Strengthener, Standby) will not come to you [into close fellowship with you]; but if I go away, I will send Him to you [to be in close fellowship with you]. And when He comes, He will convict and convince the world and bring demonstration to it about sin and about righteousness (uprightness of heart and right standing with God) and about judgment.

John 16:7–8 (AMP)

Although our Father often blesses us with success and plenty, this is no longer the differentiating mark that sets us apart from the world. Through Christ, we are now vessels that can actually house the very spirit of the living God. We can come into intimate and close fellowship with our Lord, made possible only under the new covenant. Now our peculiar and unique mark is that God's wisdom, power, and righteousness are manifested to, in, and through us. We no longer stand on the outside of the holy of holies with a visible sign from the earth; we abide in Christ and he abides in us; we make our home in him, and he in us (1 John 3:24). We stand in the very presence of our God and are marked with a divine seal (2 Corinthians 1:22).

All good things come from our Father above. I receive the rain in due season as a blessing. But it is no longer what I use to measure the favor of God on my life. Instead, am I radiating forth his fragrance and power? Can those around me see him and hear him through me? The world around us will be convicted and convinced only by the demonstration of the Holy Spirit.

Make Room for Roots

Other seeds fell on rocky ground, where they had not much soil; and at once they sprang up because they had no depth of soil. But when the sun rose, they were scorched, and because they had no root, they dried up and withered away.

Matthew 13:5–6 (AMP)

As for what was sown on thin (rocky) soil, this is he who hears the Word and at once welcomes and accepts it with joy; yet it has no real root in him, but is temporary (inconstant, lasts but a little while); and when affliction or trouble or persecution comes on account of the Word, at once he is caused to stumble [he is repelled and begins to distrust and desert Him whom he ought to trust and obey] and he falls away.

Matthew 13:20–21 (AMP)

A couple of things in these verses caught my attention. First, verse 5 says that the seeds planted on rocky soil sprang up at once "because they had no depth of soil." The word *because* just jumped out at me. Why would the *lack* of soil make them spring up quickly?

Seeds are amazing, really. With just the smallest amount of encouragement they will start to grow almost anywhere. Most of us have stopped in amazement to see a delicate flower bravely growing in a crack of seemingly endless pavement. I wrote in an earlier chapter of seeing trees hanging on to the edge of a rock cliff; it is almost startling. When certain ingredients are available, even in small amounts, seeds start to grow; it is just how God made them. And when the dirt is shallow and there is not room to grow downward—to grow roots—they will grow upward. However, verse 6 shows the results. "Because they had no root, they dried up and withered away." Shallow soil results in a short life.

Then, as I read the meaning of the rocky soil in verses 20–21, I began to ponder what the rocks represent. Normally I would have thought they represent areas of our lives that need healing or change, hurts or offenses that need to be removed. But then another thought came to mind. A couple of years ago, the Spirit began to teach me using stones as pictures of spiritual revelation. As I hiked, he would show me how some revelations can be on the surface, so to speak, and some revelations need to be unearthed. Some revelations are small, even broken off of larger understanding, while some are like a mountain. So, now, with the parable of the sower, I asked the Lord if this picture of rocks representing revelation could be applied.

This is what I see: Many in the body have a thin layer of soil. They have some ingredients for growth but not adequate amounts. Their hearts are tender, to a degree, so they quickly and gladly accept the Word given to them, but the joy and growth is short-lived. Their lack of growth is reflected because they're not digging deeper for personal understanding and revelation. The unseen revelation that lies within them as the Spirit dwells within them becomes a stumbling block—a hindrance—to increase.

Let me give an example. Perhaps someone hears the Word spoken concerning healing. Their instant reaction is joy and excitement, as the Word is refreshing and full of hope. However, if they don't spend personal time and energy studying what the Word says about healing, if they back off the subject when the Spirit begins to show them things they do not easily understand, the original Word of healing will dry up and die when trouble or persecution comes because there was no room in their hearts for the roots of the Word to go deeper.

1 Peter 2:6–8 tells of Jesus being the precious chief cornerstone to those who believe but a stumbling block to those who do not. Hebrews 1:3 and Colossians 1:19 say that Jesus is the perfect imprint and image of God, the full revelation of our Father. So each piece of revelation that comes to us by the Spirit as we daily seek to know

our Lord is a piece of the full revelation—or cornerstone—of Jesus. Our desire is to know the fullness of Christ. The only way to do this is to live in a constant state of seeking understanding and revelation by the Spirit.

Dig deep. His deep is calling to your deep. Uncover the revelations that lie hidden within his spirit, which lives within you. Make room for the roots of his Word to grow so that when trouble or affliction comes, his Word will remain strong and alive in your heart. When testing comes, which it does to all of us, do not stumble because of unbelief. Uncovering revelation of God's Word, by the Spirit, makes room for the growth we all long for and takes us from faith to faith and glory to glory.

Enjoying the Ride

You will show me the path of life; in Your presence is fullness of
joy, at Your right hand there are pleasures forevermore.
Psalm 16:11 (AMP)

Remember those long road trips back before cars had DVD players?
Remember being crammed together, five kids in the back seat, before
seatbelts were even a thought? Remember the dreaded question "Are
we there yet?" Okay, I may be dating myself a bit, but I remember
those days. My family was famous for the forty-two-hour, non-stop
marathons to Granny and Popper's house. Some people like to stop
and enjoy the sites along the way, but not us. We stopped only for
gas—use the bathroom then!—and ate sandwiches on the road. I
can laugh now, but at the time it was anything but fun for a kid.

There seem to be a lot of people right now in the body of Christ
who are so intent on "getting there" that the trip is drained of all
its fun possibilities. The work of the ministry has become more of
a job than a passion. I will quickly admit that my eyes are often set
intently on the horizon, and so I can get a little tunnel vision at
times. But I am also learning more and more that the moment by
moment details of the day breathe life into the journey.

Solomon's famous words in Ecclesiastes 3 remind us that there
is a season for everything under heaven. There is a time to be born
and a time to die. There is a time to weep and a time to laugh. And
I believe there is also a time to be focused and serious and a time
to rest and enjoy the simple pleasures that become brilliant with
the light of God shining on them. Yes, we are in the midst of the
greatest time in history, spiritually speaking. The slumbering bride

is waking and wiping the sleep from her eyes. She is filling her lamp with oil and preparing herself for a war of love. There is no time to waste, and this is no time to be frivolous with our lives or frugal with his glory. But this race is not down a dirt path with cardboard trees. It is in a kingdom of splendor and majesty, the details of which our Creator longs for us to see and enjoy.

When was the last time you ran through a puddle and laughed as the light made rainbows bounce around you? Did you notice the last time you ate an orange the way it makes your tongue tingle and then ends with a little bit of sweetness? Do you see the way birds lift on the wind almost effortlessly but then zigzag as the current seems to move them where they didn't expect? Why not go for a walk down that path you've noticed a hundred times but were too busy to explore? Why not just sit down and read that book or have a cup of hot chocolate in the middle of the routine? Our Father is one who longs for us to enjoy this journey as much as he longs for us to finish the race. Find the treasures he has strategically placed along the way just to see you smile, and you will bring him great joy.

Amy Layne Litzelman

Love without *Buts*

Once we, too, were foolish and disobedient. We were misled by others … But then God our Savior showed us his kindness and love. He saved us, not because of the good things we did, but because of his mercy. He washed away our sins and gave us a new life through the Holy Spirit.

Titus 3:3–6 (NLT)

It is so easy to look around and clump people into groups. Our society seems to thrive on categorizing and labeling to try to make sense of things. Some sad but common stereotypes are: the elderly are outdated, the poor are ignorant, Christians are boring hypocrites, immigrants just want a free ride, kids with energy have ADHD, and all teenagers are rebellious. As there must always be a basis on which to begin any thought, we could probably find examples to support each of these generalities. However, I would much rather show the countless exceptions, knowing that to speak life over someone is to call them forth to be who their Creator sees them to be.

Take teenagers, for example. I have two teenage sons and have learned priceless lessons through them as I've submitted to the Spirit's leading. It is easy to see the fashion trends in hair, clothing, piercing, tattoos, etc. and say, "Well, they're just rebellious." And, granted, many are—against parents, teachers, the law, the Church. But I heard the Spirit say to me that he has put a certain drive and ambition in each of us to move us forward and not stay stationary. He has placed a hunger inside each of us to reach out past the norm, the inconsistencies, the questions, and the contradictions within ourselves and our society. Sometimes the results are obviously positive while other times we have to look past what we perceive as negative to see what lies within the heart.

I do not advocate rebellion; I do think, however, that not all of what we perceive as rebellious is necessarily so. In fact, I wonder if sometimes we push our kids into rebellion because we label them as such when they are simply growing and trying to find out who they are and what they like. Time and again I have gone to my Father to ask if I should allow my sons to do things that looked questionable in my eyes. He said, *Let them go.*

First, they need to learn how to make decisions on their own—the good ones and the bad. They need to experience both the rewards of wisdom and the forgiveness and grace that quickly pour out from a loving Father and family in the face of error. Second, I need to trust that the faithfulness, kindness, and mercy my Father has so generously given me is just as pointedly directed at them. Our children, our friends, and our loved ones are all within the scope of his spirit at all times as he leads them to opportunities of revelation and understanding, places where their hearts are forever captured by him. Third, if we are willing to learn from those younger and different than ourselves, there are great treasures to be gained. I have again found laughter and curiosity that had somehow slipped out of my life through the need to be responsible. I once more see that there are many ways to accomplish a task, not just *my* way. And I know even more clearly the bottom line with all people: no matter what they wear or how they act, they want to be genuinely loved and cherished with no *but*s.

Just as surely as my Father has led me on this journey to know his heart and mine, he is leading those all around us. As we love extravagantly, our eyes begin to see what only the Spirit can show us: the vastness and intricacies of his plan.

Amy Layne Litzelman

Doorways of Desire

Delight yourself also in the Lord, and He will give you the desires and secret petitions of your heart.

Psalm 37:4 (AMP)

I used to respond with mixed emotions to this verse. On one hand, it sparked a hope within that my Father saw and knew my heart and would answer those secret longings I had been carrying around, even from childhood. On the other hand, I hesitated, wondering whether my aspirations were just my own or from him. How could I *know*? And so, over the years I laid down a lot of what I thought were just my own desires, not wanting to walk in selfish disobedience.

One day the Spirit began to stir me up in this area, actually rebuking me for laying down pieces of the vision God had intended for my life. Again, I was torn. I believe the Father put unique tendencies and longings and dreams in each of us, even at our conception. Some of these original desires survive even when we rebel, and they direct, to a degree, what we do and who we become. Our own selfish ambitions emerge more and more as we long after the things of this world, however, and the waters get pretty muddy. When we turn our heart back toward God and realize our own desires distracted us from his thoughts and plans for us, questions can still linger. So, how do I know if my desires line up with his?

I have learned to ask myself a few questions, believing that his spirit will show me the truth. Above all of my individual desires, what is my *one* desire? Am I *truly* willing to do whatever he asks? What if I have laid what I am longing for at his feet, but it *still* cries out from within me? If my love and desire for my Father rises up above *all* else, then I must step out in faith, believing the desire that still remains within me is from him. I must lean on him, confident that he is fully able to override my selfish desires with his own, trusting the promise of Philippians 2:13 (NLT), "For God is working in you, giving you the desire to obey him and the power to do what pleases him."

Going back to Psalm 37:4, I want to look at the condition of delighting ourselves in the Lord. There is much more to being delighted in God than just being happy with his blessings. *Ânag*, the Hebrew word used here and translated as *delight*, is a primary root meaning "to be soft or pliable."[25] What an amazing picture this is. It is what the Lord spoke of in Jeremiah 18:6b (AMP): "Behold, as the clay is in the potter's hand, so are you in My hand." We were formed in our mother's womb before our birth, and when we turn our heart toward Jesus in a second birth, we are being formed again, shaped and molded into the image of Christ, the firstborn among many brethren. As we yield, as we trust, as we rely on him, we are being conformed even more intricately into God's image in purpose, thought, and action. We received God-given desires at conception and are given more each day as we lay our lives down before him.

I want to encourage you not to quickly lay aside the thing you desire. The dream hibernating within you may be the doorway God has chosen to pour out his glory through you.

For He Spoke and It Was Done

He (*Jesus*) is the sole expression of the glory of God [the Light-being, the out-raying or radiance of the divine], and He is the perfect imprint and very image of [God's] nature, upholding and maintaining and guiding and propelling the universe by His mighty word of power.

Hebrews 1:3a (AMP)

Amy Layne Litzelman

Recently the Spirit took me back to this important truth in Hebrews. As I was pondering a personal promise from my Father that had not yet seen fulfillment, a shadow of doubt crossed my mind. In response, the Spirit asked me, *Are the stars falling from the sky?* I was taken aback as he asked again, *Are the planets falling from the heavens?*

"No."

He continued. *If even the tiniest detail of my Word is not fulfilled, then the stars and planets—which are held in place by my Word—would immediately fall from the sky. If any of my Word is not true, if any of it is not fulfilled, then none of it is true.*

There is no option but that God's Word is fulfilled; the very nature and character of our Lord insists upon it. Isaiah 55:11 is not just a light encouragement. Every word God speaks will most certainly accomplish and produce that for which he intended it; God's utterance comes into existence on the breath of his power and shall prosper in the thing for which he sent it. I don't believe it was just a coincidence when God chose the stars to relate to Abraham his promise of building a nation through him. I wonder if every time Abraham looked up at the sky, he was not encouraged that as long as those distant lights still shone down upon him, as long as they still hung in the heavens, the promise of his God stood firm.

1 Samuel 3:19–20 (AMP) says, "Samuel grew; the Lord was with him and let none of his words fall to the ground. And all Israel from Dan to Beersheba knew that Samuel was established to be a prophet of the Lord." God found in Samuel a pure vessel through which to speak his untainted word. Samuel's words did not fall to the ground because they were God's words. As I thought on these verses, a picture dropped into my spirit; I saw a word coming from the mouth of God, almost as a living cloud, roaming the earth, searching for a place a to be fulfilled. It did not rest but hovered and searched until it came to pass in the perfection with which the Creator had intended.

It has been on my heart, and I have written a lot about the importance of perseverance to complete the destiny that our Father longs for us to fulfill. But what happens when prophetic words are spoken over individuals and they choose to walk away from that destiny? I believe that one reason children are such a blessing from God is that they inherit the opportunity to be vessels to fulfill God's words which have been dismissed by former generations. Whether you are believing God for a promise in his written Word, standing in faith for a personal word whispered by his spirit to yours, or simply making yourself available to a hovering, unfulfilled prophecy, know without wavering that "the grass withers, the flower fades, but the word of our God will stand forever" (Isaiah 40:8, AMP).

> Let all the earth fear the Lord [revere and worship Him]; let all the inhabitants of the world stand in awe of Him. For He spoke, and it was done; He commanded, and it stood fast.
>
> The Lord brings the counsel of the nations to nought; He makes the thoughts and plans of the peoples of no effect. The counsel of the Lord stands forever, the thoughts of His heart through all generations.
>
> Blessed (happy, fortunate, to be envied) is the nation whose God is the Lord, the people He has chosen as his heritage.
>
> Psalm 33:8–12 (AMP)

As a side note, Isaiah 61:11 in the Amplified Bible contains a great nugget. "For as [surely as] the earth brings forth its shoots, and as the garden causes what is sown in it to spring forth, so [surely] the Lord God will cause rightness and justice and praise to spring forth before all the nations [*through the self-fulfilling power of His word*]" (emphasis mine). It is not our effort that brings forth God's promises to us. Each word of our Creator actually contains within its very core the power to fulfill itself. We are to simply believe his truths, trust in his love and wisdom towards us, and obey any instructions he gives us along the way to its reality, making us a landing pad for his plans.

Amy Layne Litzelman

To Those Who Possess
the Holy Spirit

[The purpose is] that through the church the complicated, many-sided wisdom of God in all its infinite variety and innumerable aspects might now be made known to the angelic rulers and authorities (principalities and powers) in the heavenly sphere.

Ephesians 3:10 (AMP)

My spirit has been bursting forth with the reality of the unseen future. Not just in the easy and obvious but in the impossible and seemingly foolish. Where death stares at me, I see life. Where pain pricks me, I feel joy. Where it would appear no hope can reside, unquenchable tenacity has risen up within. I cannot fully understand or explain it, but where weariness pulled on me and hope had grown thin, a strength and vision has taken a hold and won't let go. Somehow, although the physical landscape around me has not changed and the circumstances still appear grim, my spirit has begun to soar.

As I was writing in my journal on a completely different topic, a sentence burst into my mind: *Love sees with the end in focus.* Why am I suddenly able to see beyond the flat surface in front of me to an end that I cannot even understand? I believe it boils down to one thing. My Father has, once again, deepened my knowledge and experience of his love for me and in me.

There are thresholds we step over in the Spirit and are very aware of. And then there are times when we are just walking or crawling through a dark corridor, our faith and love driving us forward, when suddenly we find ourselves in a totally new dimension. Without even knowing the precise moment it happened or what exactly brought the breakthrough, we glance up, catch our breath, and know anew the depths and riches of God's love and faithfulness. Amazingly, every time we go deeper in the knowledge and experience of God's love for us, we open up new treasuries of his wisdom. Suddenly we step into new arenas of being able to birth of the Spirit, not just of the physical. What exactly does this look like? Well, there are as many facets and possibilities as grains of sand, but here is a glimpse.

I have been in groups of passionate people, all talking about God's Word and what's happening in their lives, but not all that is spoken is equal. The words of one person cause my spirit to rise and soar while another's seem to bring me back down to earth. Why? The wisdom of God resonates with the breath of God, putting wind under our wings while the wisdom of man is simply the breath of man. One builds the kingdom of God while the other promotes a limited agenda. The wisdom of God brings forth life and freedom, not suffocating boundaries and heavy yokes. It speaks forth heaven-born potential, not focusing on the enemy's limited tactics. It looks upon a broken, empty shell of a person, lost and hungry, yet sees a strong tower pulsating with destiny and purpose.

This is the complicated, many-sided wisdom of God: to see the unseen, to believe the illogical, to love the unworthy, to speak the impossible, to be carriers of his grace and peace, to walk without wavering, to desire just one thing: *his* satisfaction. When we find ourselves doing this, we have touched the edge of the mind of God and are vessels available for his glory.

> ...what we are setting forth is a wisdom of God once hidden [from the human understanding] and now revealed to us by God—[that wisdom] which God devised and decreed before the ages for our glorification [to lift us into the glory of His presence]. None of the rulers of this age or world perceived and recognized and understood this, for if they had, they would never have crucified the Lord of glory.
>
> But, on the contrary, as the Scripture says, What eye has not seen and ear has not heard and has not entered into the heart of man, [all that] God has prepared (made and keeps ready) for

those who love Him [who hold Him in affectionate reverence, promptly obeying Him and gratefully recognizing the benefits He has bestowed].

Yet to us God has unveiled and revealed them by and through His spirit, for the [Holy] Spirit searches diligently, exploring and examining everything, even sounding the profound and bottomless things of God [the divine counsels and things hidden and beyond man's scrutiny].

For what person perceives (knows and understands) what passes through a man's thoughts except the man's own spirit within him? Just so no one discerns (comes to know and comprehend) the thoughts of God except the spirit of God.

Now we have not received the spirit [that belongs to] the world, but the [Holy] Spirit who is from God, [given to us] that we might realize and comprehend and appreciate the gifts [of divine favor and blessings so freely and lavishly] bestowed on us by God. And we are setting these truths forth in words not taught by human wisdom but taught by the [Holy] Spirit, combining and interpreting spiritual truths with spiritual language [to those who possess the Holy Spirit].

1 Corinthians 2:7–13 (AMP)

Imbalance of Pressure

But will God indeed dwell with men on the earth? Behold, the heavens and heaven of heavens [in its most extended compass] cannot contain You; how much less this house that I have built?

Yet graciously consider the prayer and supplication of Your servant, O Lord my God, to hearken to the [loud] cry and prayer which he prays before You today, that Your eyes may be open toward this house night and day, toward the place of which You have said, My Name [and the token of My presence] shall be there, that You may hearken to the prayer which Your servant shall make in [or facing toward] this place.

1 Kings 8:27–29 (AMP)

I admit I have never liked science much. While growing up it seemed to consist of a lot of information I just couldn't quite grasp, so I tried to avoid it rather than dig deeper. Years later, however, while home-schooling my two sons for eleven years, it became an unavoidable area. Amazingly, I found myself being led deeper and deeper as the Spirit opened my eyes to see it from a whole new perspective.

For example, Eli and I were studying the atmosphere surrounding the earth. One thing I had never considered before is that air has mass and is pressing down on the earth with an average weight of 14.7 pounds per square inch. Depending on your size, you could have 150–200 pounds of air pressing down on each of your shoulders right now. Although there are days when we all feel like the weight of the world is resting on our shoulders, we don't really feel this atmospheric pressure because there is an equal pressure pushing on us from all sides, including from within.

Amy Layne Litzelman

Now, suppose the atmosphere is pressing down on an object, like a building, which is also full of air; the oxygen and nitrogen molecules and other gases from within are also pressing back and the building remains intact. If you were able to completely remove the air from within, however, the building would collapse because of an imbalance of molecules and, therefore, an imbalance of pressure. Basically, the outside pressure would fill the void within.

Now, follow me to the spiritual significance. There has been an increased groaning rising up from the Church for the kingdom of God to come on earth as it is in heaven. It has seemed, however, that except in a few places, instead of seeing the glory and power many have expected, we have been inundated with trials and testing. We have been shaken to our cores, seeing all that is not pure within us being stripped and burned away. We have either given up or have come into agreement with our Father for our hearts to be emptied of all but desperation to know him yet more and more. As we become empty of all that is not him, there becomes an increasing imbalance between the "pressure" from above and the "pressure" from within. At some point, this earthly vessel will be empty of self, collapse under the pressure of heaven, and be consumed with the kingdom of God. It is inevitable. It cannot be stopped.

Imagine such pure wisdom—that our Father would know the perfect way to bring his kingdom to earth. Don't grow weary. Don't give up. Our Father is faithful to complete all he has started and all he has promised. The heavens are so very heavy that sometimes it feels like a giant water balloon hanging over my head. Just think, it could give way at any moment, and *you* could be a vessel through which it pours out across the earth.

> Do not, therefore, fling away your fearless confidence, for it carries a great and glorious compensation of reward. For you have need of steadfast patience and endurance, so that you may perform and fully accomplish the will of God, and thus receive and carry away [and enjoy to the full] what is promised.
> Hebrews 10:35–36 (AMP)

Against All Odds

Sing, O barren one, you who did not bear; break forth into singing and cry aloud, you who did not travail with child! For the [spiritual] children of the desolate one will be more than the children of the married wife, says the Lord.

Enlarge the place of your tent, and let the curtains of your habitations be stretched out; spare not; lengthen your cords and strengthen your stakes, for you will spread abroad to the right hand and to the left; and your offspring will possess the nations and make the desolate cities to be inhabited.

Isaiah 54:1–3 (AMP)

There is a fire, a tenacity of soul and spirit that grabs the heart of our Maker. Sometimes this fire can be misinterpreted by on-lookers as stubbornness, but it is not necessarily contained within an obvious, outward trait, immediately recognizable to all. As it is a condition of the heart, a resolution beyond words to express, it may remain hidden deep within, or it may spill out in emotions and actions. Either way, it is unmistakable to our Father above.

Think about the picture painted in the verses above: a barren woman; a woman who has tried again and again to conceive but with no success; a woman who appears to be out of God's favor; a woman who must deal daily with the humiliation that she has failed to reach her dreams and desires, a part of her very reason for living, and there is absolutely nothing she can do to change it.

But she just can't get away from those words, "Sell everything and buy the field" (Matthew 13:44). Isn't that the risk God has asked her to take: to step past the countless tears and questions; to get beyond the logic and arguments; to believe one more time. And not only to believe but to sing, to celebrate, to enlarge her home in preparation of coming children, to the shaking heads of the neighbors. That's a *lot* to ask when a heart has grown weary. And yet he asks because he is looking, searching, for a heart with that fire, that tenacity, that willingness.

That's a huge word, an expensive word: *willingness.*

Willing to step into the dark.

Willing to step through the fear.

Willing to step over the pain.

Willing to risk it all, sell it all, or give it all away at his word.

This isn't just a casual attitude. *Webster's New World Thesaurus* lists some synonyms for *willing/willingness:* "zealous, enthusiastic, eager, reliable, prompt, obedient, responsible, agreeable, prepared, voluntary, and ready."[26] I would like to add that this willingness sometimes comes in a place of great weariness or confusion, but the heart cry is still the same. *Yes, Father, at your word.*

Think of Mary's words in Luke 1:38 (AMP), "Behold, I am the handmaiden of the Lord; let it be done to me according to what you have said." This young virgin suddenly found herself in the midst of an absolutely stupendous situation, and yet, willingness so filled her heart that she believed beyond all sense of logic that she would birth the Son of God.

When we say, "Yes, Father," we silence the voices that try to bring doubt. When we say, "Yes, Father," we believe that one voice can override all others. When we say, "Yes, Father," we believe that that one voice will speak only truth.

Over and over the Bible records Jesus searching for this same mixture of desperation, perseverance, and faith. It caused Nicodemus to climb a tree. It pushed Peter to throw the net out again and to walk on water. This willingness to try again resulted in blind eyes opening, lame feet walking, the Centurion's absent daughter being healed, and demoniacs being set free. In one Gentile woman, this fire was not dampened even when Jesus told her that he was sent only to help the people of Israel. As she worshiped and pleaded again, Jesus responded to her great faith, stepped for a moment beyond his boundaries, and healed her daughter.

The path to our future is not always smooth. In fact, if our heart burns for him, it will most certainly lead us through many deep valleys and up many steep mountainsides. But the promise of our Father is sure. The children of the barren woman will be more than the married wife, and they will possess the nations to make them fruitful. The shame of our youth, the area of our humiliation, and the place of our emptiness will become our glory.

The Esther Anointing

Then the king held out to Esther the golden scepter. So Esther arose and stood before the king. And she said, If it pleases the king and if I have found favor in his sight and the thing seems right before the king and I am pleasing to his eyes, let it be written to reverse the letters devised by Haman son of Hammedatha, the Agagite, which he wrote to destroy the Jews who are in all the king's provinces. For how can I endure to see the evil that shall come upon my people? Or how can I endure to see the destruction of my kindred?

Esther 8:4–6 (AMP)

Early one morning I awoke to the sound of Todd Bentley's CD *Marinating*, which had been playing beside my bed all night. As I lay in the dark, in the sweetness of God's presence, "The Esther Anointing" began to play. As I soaked in the music, scriptures, and prayers asking to be immersed in the oils and perfumes of God's presence, the Spirit asked me, *What is your request?* Before my mind had time to think or respond, my spirit leapt within me and said, *Freedom for my people.*

Suddenly, my mind caught up with my heart and I realized the significance of my request. As I had talked with friends and acquaintances, it was unmistakable that almost all had just been through the most difficult yet most significant years of their lives. Circumstances, though greatly varied, had brought each one to their weakest before their Lord and yet had also taken each to a greater revelation and new strength in his love and grace. From the depths of despair and pain, the body is beginning to arise to new heights of faith and trust. Just like Esther, we have been going through an intense cleansing and purification. Now, stirring up within our spirits is a deep cry of "Freedom" for those around us.

Freedom for the angry.

Freedom for the addicted.

Freedom for the weary.

Freedom for the abused.

Freedom!

Everywhere I look I see people bound by lies and deception, people who are stuck in destructive mindsets and circumstances, people who are hurt and dying. But Jesus has given us the request of our hearts, the key to set the captives free. Only believe. If I believe in his goodness, if I believe in his wisdom and power, if I truly believe the words he has spoken—and is still speaking—these faith-ignited words will reverse and redeem the captivity around me.

Have you also gone through a season of stripping away and cleansing? Draw close to your Lord. Draw close and soak in his love and faithfulness. Let him strengthen your heart with his. Then go and proclaim the freedom he has purchased with his own life. Not only does our God exist, but he rewards those who earnestly seek him out (Hebrews 11:6). Proclaim it, believe it, and watch the world around you change.

"In the time of their suffering when they cried to You, You heard them from heaven, and according to Your abundant mercy You gave them deliverers, who saved them from their enemies" (Nehemiah 9:27b, AMP).

He Knows

Nothing in all creation can hide from him. Everything is naked
and exposed before his eyes.

Hebrews 4:13a (NLT)

It doesn't take long in our walk with God to see how vast and detailed
his plans are—how he truly *does* know all things. Unless we are trying not to see, it really jumps out at every turn. People connections,
time connections, details the world writes off as coincidences start to
reveal themselves for what they really are: the mighty hand of God.

Our Father is not sitting in heaven wondering what is going
to happen next. It is a great mystery and hard to wrap our understanding around, but to him all of what we are living right now has
already happened. He has already seen it, from beginning to end.
This doesn't mean it has all been scripted and we have no say or
choice in the matter. It just means that he is all-knowing and knows
what we are going to decide before we do. He knows what tomorrow
holds before it comes because he sits above time and space. Furthermore, he sees through the obvious, surface-level particulars to
the deepest unseen core. He knows the intricate make-up of every
cell and atom, even every thought and motive. He knows how they
come together in order to build, and how they break down with the
intent to destroy.

As I was walking one day, the Spirit gave me just the briefest
glimpse of this truth. I was enjoying the cool, spring day, noticing the new green growth and listening to the birds sing. My spirit
welled up within me as I saw how complex his creation was and
how it all worked together so perfectly from season to season. Sud-

denly my eyes opened to see not only the earth before me but the earth below me. It is hard to put into words, but it was as if the ground opened under my feet and I could see in great detail what was normally unseen but of vast importance to what was happening on the surface. I saw countless roots pulling in moisture and nutrients. Ants, worms, and other insects all performed God-given tasks. Water droplets traveled down millions of tiny pathways around layers of dirt, sediment, and rock. Deeper still was the very core of the earth, vastly unknown to us and yet of such importance to our very existence.

The vision was very brief, yet revealing. Below our feet lies a sort of hidden, and many times forgotten, world of its own. These details are in absolute full view to our Creator, however. In the same way, every seemingly hidden portion of our lives stands as in an open field before our Lord. He knows. He sees. And he cares. Not one thought goes unnoticed. Not one cry unheard. Not one word unrecorded. Both our needs and desires stand in full view before our Lord, and if we are quiet, if we are listening, he will give us direction and understanding in all of these things. He will tell us his hidden design, his purposes and plans, and ask us to join him in these coming to pass—for us and through us. "He holds in his hands the depths of the earth and the mightiest mountains" (Psalm 95:4a, NLT).

Passing through the Valley of Weeping

Blessed (happy, fortunate, to be envied) is the man whose strength is in You, in whose heart are the highways to Zion. Passing through the Valley of Weeping (Baca), they make it a place of springs; the early rain also fills [the pools] with blessings. They go from strength to strength [increasing in victorious power]; each of them appears before God in Zion. O Lord God of hosts, hear my prayer; give ear, O God of Jacob!

Psalm 84:5–8 (AMP)

Amy Layne Litzelman

I don't know that I would have ever considered myself a crier. I know some people who seem to cry at the drop of a hat, tender at every turn. I did not have a problem being touched emotionally, but I just don't remember weeping a lot when I was younger. Well, that has changed somewhat.

There is a place on the road to God's increasing presence called the Valley of Weeping. Experienced here are depths of sorrow and compassion formerly unknown. This is not a gender-specific experience; I have talked to both men and women who have trekked through this same valley and the stories are consistent. *Oh God, will this pain ever stop? Will these tears ever cease?*

Verse 5 (above) says the man on this journey is blessed, fortunate, and to be envied. This is indeed true, but the blessing is not always so evident, so distinguishable, in the midst. That is why God's Word and those who have gone before are so invaluable. Look again at Psalm 84 (*abbreviated*):

> Blessed is the man whose strength is in You, in whose heart are the highways to Zion. Passing through the Valley of Weeping, they make it a place of springs; the early rain also fills the pools with blessings. They go from strength to strength, increasing in victorious power; each of them appears before God in Zion.

First, blessed is the man whose strength is in his God. How we struggle with our weaknesses. How we analyze them and roll them around in our minds. And yet, our Creator not only knew we were going to be weak, he made radical provision for it *in himself.*

> But He said to me, My grace (My favor and loving-kindness and mercy) is enough for you [sufficient against any danger and enables you to bear the trouble manfully]; for My strength and power are made perfect (fulfilled and completed) and show themselves most effective in [your] weakness. Therefore, I will all the more gladly glory in my weaknesses and infirmities, that the strength and power of Christ (the Messiah) may rest (yes, may pitch a tent over and dwell) upon me!
>
> 2 Corinthians 12:9 (AMP)

[For He] is not weak and feeble in dealing with you, but is a mighty power within you; for though He was crucified in weakness, yet He goes on living by the power of God. And though we too are weak in Him [as He was humanly weak], yet in dealing with you [we shall show ourselves] alive and strong in [fellowship with] Him by the power of God.

2 Corinthians 13:3b-4 (AMP)

And what shall I say further? For time would fail me to tell of Gideon, Barak, Samson, Jephthah, of David and Samuel and the prophets, who by [the help of] faith subdued kingdoms, administered justice, obtained promised blessings, closed the mouths of lions, extinguished the power of raging fire, escaped the devourings of the sword, out of frailty and weakness won strength and became stalwart, even mighty and resistless in battle, routing alien hosts.

Hebrews 11:32–34 (AMP)

Notice that Hebrews 11:33 says, "By the help of faith" these feats were accomplished. How do we deal with our weaknesses? How do we get beyond our frailty? How can we invoke the favor and blessing of our Father? By taking our eyes away from ourselves and putting our faith in the one who has chosen to house his strength within us.

Second, Psalm 84 tells us that God's blessing falls on the one whose heart contains the highways to Zion. What does this mean? It means that God has put a yearning within us to meet with him, a beckoning that is overwhelming. I have a friend who loves to ride motorcycles, and come the first warm, spring day, the road silently summons him; it is irresistible. Once we have tasted of God's goodness, once we have seen his glorious ways, we are drawn further and further into him; *he* is irresistible.

So, having God's strength and this unquenchable yearning within us, we suddenly find ourselves in this Valley of Weeping. This doesn't seem like a great reward. Yet, hidden here are treasures found nowhere else on the journey. Something about the combination of tears and faith unearths hidden springs in the Spirit. Not tears of self-pity or selfish ambition; these seem to only put us in a dry pit.

Amy Layne Litzelman

But those who cry out with faith in God's love and goodness will soon find themselves standing in water. And just as water in the natural environment evaporates up only to eventually rain down, so too will these hidden springs and tears soon bring the rain from above.

Oh Lord God, hear our prayers. See our yearning and do what so fills your heart to do. Refresh us with hidden springs, take us to new levels of your strength, and bring us into your chambers.

Voluntary Altars—
Perpetual Praise

He is your praise; He is your God, Who has done for you these
great and terrible things which your eyes have seen.

Deuteronomy 10:21 (AMP)

Amy Layne Litzelman

Have you ever had a distinct God encounter that deserves to be marked by some sort of an altar or monument? Some altars in the Bible were built in accordance to God's specific instructions and plans. Others, however, were voluntary altars of worship. These were built by hearts that had heard God's voice and experienced his radical provision, protection, and faithfulness.

Jacob set up many such pillars over the years: when he saw the ladder between earth and heaven and heard God speak again the promises given to his father, Abraham; when he returned safely to Succoth with his wives and family after meeting with Esau, his brother; when God spoke to him and gave him a new name, Israel; and when Rachel died.

After nearly 100 years of building an ark in the face of ridicule and another year floating on the waters, I can only imagine all of the emotions that flooded out of Noah and his family as they knelt again on dry ground. Noah immediately built an altar to honor the one who had been faithful to keep them.

On an early morning walk I was talking with my Father. I was so overcome by his love and his specific and personal promise of freedom and healing to me that I knelt by the path and built a small monument of love in return. A week later I passed the same place and thought again of his love and gentleness. I started to go and kneel again to worship when the Spirit clearly spoke to me. He explained that since the moment I had built the altar, the altar itself had been worshiping for the very thing for which it had been built. All of creation praises and worships the Creator already, but when we pile up rocks or other objects as an altar of worship, these objects come into agreement on that point and the worship never ceases, day or night, to the one whom we adore.

What an amazing thought. How great is the power of unity and agreement. May we as the body of Christ be an altar of living stones in unity and worship to the Son, Christ Jesus, and to our Father.

A Lover's Delight

Your people will offer themselves willingly in the day of Your power, in the beauty of holiness and in holy array out of the womb of the morning; to You [will spring forth] Your young men, who are as the dew.

Psalm 110:3 (AMP)

One summer evening I attended an amazing concert, *Chicago Style Jazz, Straight Up*. Five musicians joined their award-winning talent and their love for jazz to soar far above where most musicians have walked. Over and over they seemed to pull from each other new sounds and rhythms. Their pure joy in the process was contagious to most all who were watching. But just as contagious in my eyes was a young lady sitting directly in front of me. I noticed by her posture and movement to the beat that she was enjoying the concert. Then, when the musicians would erupt with spontaneous dips and turns, she would burst out with laughter and clap with delight. She saw and heard little nuances that others around her might have briefly noticed but not truly appreciated if her enthusiasm had not pointed them out. It became more and more apparent that she both knew and loved jazz; this was not an outsider's admiration but a lover's delight.

Have you met believers like this? They don't stand at a distance and admire who God is and what he does; they sit on the edge of their seats in anticipation because they know him and delight in his ways. When his wisdom causes circumstances to take sudden, unexpected turns, they watch with excitement. When he speaks in ways unforeseen, these lovers of his Word seem to sink down into the

Amy Layne Litzelman

midst of him and soak it in. I love being around people like this. It makes me hungry. It makes me dig deeper. It makes me look harder and run farther. Their delight, their joy, their pure love and passion are contagious to any who can receive it.

I think of David and the sons of Korah, writers of most of the Biblical psalms. Even through the valleys of despair and confusion, their urgent cries of love and hope rose up from within, sure of the one of whom they sang. It is no wonder that most of us don't go very long without finding ourselves back in this book. Their words of intimate exaltation draw us up, closer into the Father's lap.

When we see the power of a contagious heart, we can more easily understand the decisive nature of Jesus's words in Matthew 22:37 (AMP), "You shall love the Lord your God with all your heart and with all your soul and with all your mind (intellect)." As we experience and realize the flow of God's love toward us, we won't be able to contain our love in return to him. What power and passion flows forth through one who truly knows their God!

You know, we can quote the written Word all day to our friends, but nothing will touch them like our own hunger and love for the Word himself. It is not dutiful love that attracts but love freely lavished from a heart familiar with the gardens of heaven.

Beyond the Wonder of a Dream

And if you pour out that with which you sustain your own life for the hungry and satisfy the need of the afflicted, then shall your light rise in darkness, and your obscurity and gloom become like the noonday. And the Lord shall guide you continually and satisfy you in drought and dry places and make strong your bones.

And you shall be like a watered garden and like a spring of water whose waters fail not. And your ancient ruins shall be rebuilt; you shall raise up the foundations of [buildings that have laid waste for] many generations; and you shall be called Repairer of the Breach, Restorer of Streets to Dwell In.

Isaiah 58:10–12 (AMP)

Somewhere, somehow
I'll see your glory risin' over me and fulfilling
Your dream to show your grace to all the world
Through your love, through your Son
Through your wisdom in my weakness
Somewhere and somehow
You'll pour your glory out just like the sea

Somewhere and somehow
Your light will shine for all the world to see and to know hope
That rests beyond the wonder of a dream

Amy Layne Litzelman

From your heart, from your hand
To the very core of man
Somewhere and somehow
You'll shine your light across this barren land

Come fulfill your dream in me
The power of love to set man free
Displayed for all the earth to see
A broken vessel I will be

Somewhere and somehow
The love that conquered death will truly be known—will be shown
Through those who bear the Name, who wear the scars
Of a life laid before
A King we worship and adore
Somewhere, somehow
The world will know that you and I are one

Humble Places of Love

Behold my Servant, whom I uphold, My elect in Whom My soul delights! I have put My Spirit upon Him; He will bring forth justice and right and reveal truth to the nations. He will not cry or shout aloud or cause His voice to be heard in the street. A bruised reed He will not break, and a dimly burning wick He will not quench; He will bring forth justice in truth. He will not fail or become weak or be crushed and discouraged till He has established justice in the earth; and the islands and coastal regions shall wait hopefully for Him and expect His direction and law.

Isaiah 42:1–4 (AMP)

But I will sing of Your mighty strength and power; yes, I will sing aloud of Your mercy and loving-kindness in the morning; for You have been to me a defense (a fortress and a high tower) and a refuge in the day of my distress.

Psalm 59:16 (AMP)

I had the most amazing dream. Never have I felt or experienced such glory in my sleep. Even remembering and writing this now touches a tender, intimate place within me, echoing a call deep from my Father's heart. I did not dream of going to heaven, but rather, of seeing heaven come down.

I was in a large room, in a gathering of people I did not know. Several rows of chairs lined the walls while rows of round tables filled in the center of the room. A master of ceremonies walked among the crowd, choosing individuals in order to spotlight their accomplishments. Sometimes he would point out someone and then articulate their achievements; other times he would call on them to personally share. The crowd would erupt in applause as each one told stories of building great organizations around the world. I remember one young man sitting across the table from me. His appearance radiated success. He sat up confidently as he relayed the many activities he had been involved in and their obvious benefits. It was impressive, to be sure, but somehow it did not touch my spirit.

Then, without warning, the host turned and spoke to a man sitting, hidden, in the corner near me. In a rather mocking way, the speaker said, "And you—it is good to see you are awake and made it. What have you accomplished?" From the second row, a weary, ruffled man stepped forward. A murmur of quiet amusement moved through the room. In a muted voice, without lifting his eyes, the weathered man began to recite a list of very common activities. He had, in fact, woken up that day; he had done his chores; he had fed the animals and brought in the hay; he had carried in the firewood and cleaned his home. His list was simple, and yet something touched a spark to my spirit. As I continued to listen, the spark within me burst into a blaze. Without thought of anyone around me, I stood up, moved into the aisle in front of this man, and began to clap. He looked up, surprised, but continued on, quietly telling not what he had achieved, but that he had left all behind, had laid down his dreams, and had stayed home to care for his responsibilities. The flame inside me grew and, without premeditation, I found myself now cheering and whistling. As I sat on the edge of my table, rocking it in enthusiastic praise, the crowd around me seemed to awaken and join in, not really understanding why they were clapping.

As I continued to salute this hidden hero, I saw weariness drain from his eyes. Wrinkles lifted from his face and his posture straightened. Within minutes, a young, vibrant man stood before me. His tired, ashamed voice now shifted to confidence as his mind cleared to understand the truth and importance of what he had done. In a firm, gentle tone, he said, "I stayed home to save the farm." Then, heaven opened up directly over us, and God himself smiled down with pride at his son. Angels also gathered to marvel at the one who had grabbed his Father's attention. Again, uncontrollable admiration flowed from me.

Amy Layne Litzelman

When I awoke, I laid perfectly still, hardly able to breathe. I didn't want to move and lose the glory I had felt and seen in my sleep. As I soaked in the memory of this man's weariness being so perfectly replaced with hope and life, the Spirit brought to mind Isaiah 40:31 (AMP):

> But those who wait for the Lord [who expect, look for, and hope in Him] shall change and renew their strength and power; they shall lift their wings and mount up [close to God] as eagles [mount up to the sun]; they shall run and not be weary, they shall walk and not faint or become tired.

Here had been a room full of what appeared to be very successful people. They were strong, rested, good-looking, and talented. They were motivated and confident. And they were recognized by their peers for these assets. There was one, however, who was ridiculed by men and yet honored by God. One who appeared weak and failing—and believed himself to be so—and yet shook the corridors of heaven and brought the attention of angelic hosts. One who had begun to think he was in a prison but really dwelt in the fortress and refuge of his Father.

The exquisite love of our God sees to the roots below both accomplishments *and* weariness; he divides soul and spirit to see the truth of the heart. He applauds purity of love, even when hidden in a tired vessel, and in this understanding releases justice and strength. This exhausted farmer had dreams of grandeur on behalf of his Lord, and yet he was driven by love to lay it down as the Spirit led him to stay home. After a long, dusty season, he didn't recognize the nobility of his humble task. He had given up his own life to keep something else alive. As this faithful vessel of glory waited upon his Father, they were made one, and his Father's promise of restoration and strength soon overtook him.

The word *wait* in Isaiah 40:31 is translated from the Hebrew word *qâvâh*. It is a primary root word meaning "to bind together (perhaps by twisting)." Figuratively, it also means "to expect."[27] It seems to imply two simultaneous actions: a binding together during a season of waiting for an expected promise to be fulfilled. There is no binding together, no promise, more important to our Father than that of us being one with him. This is the heart cry of Jesus in John 17; he gave his life that we might truly know our Father and rest in him, and him in us.

Many have given themselves to the Spirit, allowing him to form the ideal servant of the Lord in them. This is a costly, difficult journey. It doesn't look glitzy or impressive. It leaves scars and wrinkles. But for those who persevere, for those who continue to believe in the goodness and love of their Father, even when they question their own inadequacies, the heavens open and come down. In an instant, weariness drains away. In a moment, clouds of condemnation evaporate. Waning hope is restored and visions that lie deep within receive new fire from the altar. Then will step forth strong, prepared sons and daughters of the Most High, full of truth and justice. In contrast to earthly glory and fame, this radiance from above will leave the world stunned. We have not seen true achievements until we see what the Spirit will do through these.

No longer should we applaud what has its strength and roots in humanity. No longer should we be impressed by what is accomplished by just hard work and tenacity. Instead, let us bend low to see those who rest humbly before their Maker, willing to be doorkeepers for their Beloved. Then let the Spirit rise within us and cheer for the weary. Let our praise wash over the wounded and release them from their heaviness. Let us look up and see where heaven gathers, for our Father still glories in pouring himself out in humble places of love.

If Not for You

One thing have I asked of the Lord, that will I seek, inquire for, and [insistently] require: that I may dwell in the house of the Lord [in His presence] all the days of my life, to behold and gaze upon the beauty [the sweet attractiveness and the delightful loveliness] of the Lord and to meditate, consider, and inquire in His temple.

Psalm 27:4 (AMP)

My soul, wait only upon God and silently submit to Him; for my hope and expectation are from Him.

Psalm 62:5 (AMP)

Up mountain paths, by ancient maps
Straight to my heart you go
To search and find the hidden things
That only you would know

Great treasures deep, which lie beneath
The surface of my soul
Must be brought forth by heat and force
At just the perfect hour

If not for you I would not know
How sweet this midnight hour
When whispered words and gentle touch
My joy and strength restore

Now come again and lead me back
To quiet pastures, green
Where hope believes and faith receives
What eye has yet to see

Come sweet friend, let's dine again
Upon your words of grace
And speak of love still yet to come
In ever-increasing ways

If not for you I would not know
How sweet this midnight hour
When whispered words and gentle touch
My joy and strength restore

Amy Layne Litzelman

Endnotes

1   Funk & Wagnalls. 1980. *Standard Desk Dictionary*. Lippincott & Crowell, Publishers. 138.

2   Edwards, Betty. 1989. *Drawing on the Right Side of the Brain*. Tarcher/Putnam, New York.

3   Funk & Wagnalls. 1980. *Standard Desk Dictionary*. Lippincott & Crowell, Publishers. 720.

4   Mel Gibson, 2004. Icon Productions. Newmarket Films.

5   Peers, E. Allison. 1953. *The Complete Works of Saint John of the Cross, Doctor of the Church*. Westminster, MD: Newman Press.

6   Strong, James, LL.D., S.T.D. 1995. *The New Strong's Exhaustive Concordance of the Bible*. Nashville, TN: Thomas Nelson Publishers, Inc. 262.

7   Hurnard, Hannah. 1975. *Hind's Feet on High Places*. Wheaton, IL: Tyndale House Publishers, Inc. 138.

8   Strong, James, LL.D., S.T.D. 1995. *The New Strong's Exhaustive Concordance of the Bible*. Nashville, TN: Thomas Nelson Publishers, Inc. 385.

9   Funk & Wagnalls. 1980. *Standard Desk Dictionary*. Lippincott & Crowell, Publishers. 489.

10 Strong, James, LL.D., S.T.D. 1995. *The New Strong's Exhaustive Concordance of the Bible*. Nashville, TN: Thomas Nelson Publishers, Inc. 19.

11 Strong, James, LL.D., S.T.D. 1995. *The New Strong's Exhaustive Concordance of the Bible*. Nashville, TN: Thomas Nelson Publishers, Inc. 1159.

12   Strong, James, LL.D., S.T.D. 1995. *The New Strong's Exhaustive Concordance of the Bible*. Nashville, TN: Thomas Nelson Publishers, Inc. 1209.

13   Alle, John Gage, Phd. *Webster's Encyclopedia of Dictionaries*. 1981. Baltimore, MD: Ottenheimer Publishers, Inc. 383.

14   Alle, John Gage, Phd. *Webster's Encyclopedia of Dictionaries*. 1981. Baltimore, MD: Ottenheimer Publishers, Inc. 275.

15   Alle, John Gage, Phd. *Webster's Encyclopedia of Dictionaries*. 1981. Baltimore, MD: Ottenheimer Publishers, Inc. 275.

16   Alle, John Gage, Phd. *Webster's Encyclopedia of Dictionaries*. 1981. Baltimore, MD: Ottenheimer Publishers, Inc. 368.

17   Alle, John Gage, Phd. *Webster's Encyclopedia of Dictionaries*. 1981. Baltimore, MD: Ottenheimer Publishers, Inc. 363.

18   Strong, James, LL.D., S.T.D. 1995. *The New Strong's Exhaustive Concordance of the Bible*. Nashville, TN: Thomas Nelson Publishers, Inc. 619.

19   Strong, James, LL.D., S.T.D. 1995. *The New Strong's Exhaustive Concordance of the Bible*. Nashville, TN: Thomas Nelson Publishers, Inc. 291.

20   Strong, James, LL.D., S.T.D. 1995. *The New Strong's Exhaustive Concordance of the Bible*. Nashville, TN: Thomas Nelson Publishers, Inc. 588.

21   Strong, James, LL.D., S.T.D. 1995. *The New Strong's Exhaustive Concordance of the Bible*. Nashville, TN: Thomas Nelson Publishers, Inc. 1229.

22   *Jackson Hole Daily*. April 8, 2006. 1.

23   McPherson, Joyce. 2003. *River of Grace–A Story of John Calvin*. Lebanon, TN: Greenleaf Press. 99–100.

24   Frangipane, Francis. 2006. *The Three Battlegrounds*. Cedar Rapids, IA: Arrow Publications, Inc. 17.

25   Strong, James, LL.D., S.T.D. 1995. *The New Strong's Exhaustive Concordance of the Bible*. Nashville, TN: Thomas Nelson Publishers, Inc. 293.

26   Laird, Charlton. 1974. *Webster's New World Thesaurus*. USA: Fawcett Popular Library. 501.

27   Strong, James, LL.D., S.T.D. 1995. *The New Strong's Exhaustive Concordance of the Bible*. Nashville, TN: Thomas Nelson Publishers, Inc. 1423.